MOONCAKE COOKBOOK FOR BEGINNERS

100 EASY AND INTERESTING TREATS RECIPES FOR BEGINNERS | TIPS AND TRICKS TO MAKE PERFECT AND DELICIOUS MOONCAKES

TABLE OF CONTENTS

INTRODUCTION 5
    THE METHODS AND TECHNIQUES 5
    KEY TOOLS 7
    HOW TO STORE 8
    TIPS AND TRICKS FOR GETTING THE BEST 8

CHAPTER 1: SWEET MOONCAKES RECIPES 9
    1. FRUITS MOONCAKES 9
    2. JELLY MOONCAKES 10
    3. CHOCOLATE MOONCAKES 11
    4. MIXED NUTS MOONCAKE 12
    5. RED BEAN MOONCAKES 13
    6. TARO COCONUT SNOWY MOONCAKES 15
    7. HONEY PISTACHIO MOONCAKE 17
    8. PLUM BLOSSOM MOONCAKES 18
    9. LOTUS SEED PASTE MOONCAKES 19
    10. OREO MOONCAKES 20
    11. VIETNAMESE MOONCAKES 20
    12. DURIAN MOONCAKES 22
    13. LAVA CUSTARD MOONCAKES 23
    14. ICE-CREAM MOONCAKES 24
    15. PINEAPPLE FILLED GLUTEN-FREE MOONCAKES 25
    16. CLASSIC MANGO MOCHI 26
    17. PLUM BLOSSOM MOONCAKE 27
    18. APPLE SHAPED STEAMED BUNS MOONCAKE 27
    19. BUTTERFLY PEA MOONCAKE 28
    20. CHRYSANTHEMUM MOONCAKES 29

CHAPTER 2: EASY MOONCAKES RECIPES 30
    21. HAM MOONCAKES 30
    22. BLUE PEA FLOWER MOONCAKES 31
    23. MINI LOTUS MOONCAKES 32
    24. SNOW SKIN CUSTARD MOONCAKES 32
    25. MINCED PORK MEAT MOONCAKES 33

26.	White Lotus Mooncakes	34
27.	Mini Snow Skin Mooncakes	35
28.	Salted Egg Yolk Mooncake	37
29.	Chicken Floss Mooncake	38
30.	Cream Cheese Mooncake	38
31.	Fish Doll Mooncake	39
32.	Coffee Snow Skin Mooncakes	40
33.	Tiramisu Lotus Paste Mooncakes	41
34.	Chocolate Chip Mooncake	42
35.	Strawberry Snow Skin Mooncakes	43
36.	Crystal Flower Mooncake	44
37.	Coffee Snow Skin Chocolate Mooncake	45
38.	Pecan Mooncake	47
39.	Vanilla Mooncake	47
40.	Lotus Flower Mooncake	48

CHAPTER 3: MODERN MOONCAKES RECIPES 50

41.	No-Bake Mooncakes	50
42.	Seafood Mooncakes	51
43.	Crystal Skin Mooncakes	53
44.	Snow Skin Mooncakes	53
45.	Carrot Mooncakes	54
46.	Green Tea Mooncakes	55
47.	Multi-Grain Mooncakes	56
48.	Ferrero Rocher Brownie	56
49.	Salted Egg Yolk Custard Mooncakes	57
50.	Black Sesame Mooncakes	58
51.	Almonds Mooncakes	59
52.	Colorful Snow Skin Mooncakes	60
53.	Rainbow Soda Snow Skin Mooncakes	62
54.	Mini Snow Skin Mooncakes	62
55.	Banana Mooncakes	63
56.	Thousand Layer Mooncakes	64
57.	Pork Filled Chinese Mooncakes	65
58.	Apple Pecan Spring Roll Mooncakes	66

59.	Plain Lotus Paste With Salted Egg yolk	67
60.	Charcoal Bamboo Mooncakes	68
61.	Orange Mooncakes	70

CHAPTER 4: TRADITIONAL MOONCAKES RECIPES 72

62.	Thermomix Traditional Mooncakes	72
63.	Halal Mooncakes	72
64.	Yunnan Mooncakes	74
65.	Sakura Snow Skin Mooncakes	75
66.	Shanghainese Mooncakes	75
67.	Hopia Mooncakes	76
68.	Suzhou Style Mooncakes	77
69.	Teochew Mooncakes	78
70.	Taiwanese Mooncakes	79
71.	Cantonese-Style Mooncakes	81
72.	Matcha Coconut Custard Mooncakes	81
73.	Adzuki Mooncakes	82
74.	Maple Nuts Mooncakes	83
75.	Sushi White Mooncakes	84
76.	Dried Fruit And Nutty Mooncakes	86
77.	Savory Preparation Pork Mooncakes	88

CHAPTER 5: JAPANESE MOONCAKES RECIPE 90

78.	Mochi Mooncakes	90
79.	Matcha Snow White Mooncakes	92
80.	Lychee Martini Snow Skin Mooncakes	92
81.	Mung Bean Mooncakes	93
82.	Kiwi Fruit Mooncakes	94
83.	Piggy Snow Skin Mooncakes	95
84.	Fuzhou Dou Yong Mooncakes	96
85.	Japanesque Green Tea Mooncakes	96
86.	Warabi Mochi Mooncakes	97
87.	Chidori Manju Mooncakes	99
88.	Vegan Snow Skin Mochi Mooncakes	99
89.	Keto Mooncakes	101
90.	Wagashi Mooncakes	102

91.	Pandan Spiral Mooncakes	102
92.	Sweet Potato Mooncakes	103
93.	Jelly With Coconut Mooncakes	104
94.	Mung Bean Mooncakes	105
95.	Tsukimi Mooncakes	105
96.	Taiyaki Mooncakes	106
97.	Clipper Earl Mooncakes	107
98.	Rice Mooncakes	109
99.	Red Bean Bun Mooncakes	109
100.	Shiroan Mooncakes	110

CONCLUSION 112

INTRODUCTION

Moon cakes are a Chinese bakery product traditionally eaten during the Mid-Autumn Festival. The festival is about giving appreciation and watching the moon. Mooncakes are also regarded as a delicacy.

In Chinese culture, roundness means completeness and togetherness. A full moon indicates prosperity and reunion for the whole family. Mooncakes are sweet treats with a flaky, slightly sweet crust filled with a thick red bean or lotus seed paste.

Mooncakes are not difficult to make; however, some uncommon ingredients could be harder to find, such as golden syrup and lye water. These are both easy, and you can make them at home. Brief instructions include the method and techniques.

THE METHODS AND TECHNIQUES

Although each Mooncakes recipe below calls for a different flavor of cake and bread and offers various decorating tricks and styles, the basic steps used to create the mooncakes will be the same. You can make it home if you don't have golden syrup and lye water for mooncakes.

Prepare the Golden Syrup:

Golden syrup is an inverted sugar that we can use in various baking dishes. The mooncake recipe will require 75g of golden syrup.

Ingredients:

- One medium stainless-steel pot
- 200 g granulated sugar
- 60 g water
- 25 g lemon juice, approximately one-quarter of a lemon
- One jar

Directions:

1. Mix granulated sugar and water inside a medium pot, stir to dissolve the sugar, and heat over moderate heat until boiling.
2. Pour lemon juice and the remaining lemon peel once the syrup caramelizes and changes color. The lemons acid stops caramelization and reacts with converted solutions into inverted syrup. At this point, there's no nee need to stir the solution. Bring to a simmer for approximately 30-40minutes.
3. After 30 minutes, check the syrup's consistency with a wooden spoon by dipping the spoon into the solution, and one of the drops falls onto a plate. If the syrup spreads sometimes but holds its shape, it is ready. It is overcooked if it spreads out but does not spread at all. The water evaporates quickly at high heat. This could happen. Add some hot water to the pot a couple of tablespoons at a time until the desired consistency is reached.

4. Remove the pot from heat and allow it to cool. Once cooled, the syrup should be thicker and stored in a jar.

Make the Lye Water:

Lye water is an alkaline solution that is essentially baking soda and water. A mooncake's recipe requires 2 g of lye water.

Ingredients:

- One baking pan/tray
- Aluminum foil
- 1 tsp. baking soda
- 4 tsp. water

Directions:

1. Keep the oven temperature to 120°C
2. Cover the baking pan or tray with aluminum foil with baking soda spread on top. Bake the baking soda for 1 hour. When it's ready, remove and keep it in an airtight container. This prevents it from absorbing moisture. You can bake more to save for future use.
3. Add 1 tsp. of the baked baking soda to 4 tsp. water to make the solution. This will make it approximately 2 g of lye water.

Make the Mooncake Fillings:

There are different fillings you can use to make your mooncakes. Some Asian grocery stores sell ready-made fillers you could buy, so you can get them from the store instead of making this filling. Some are red bean, lotus seed paste, black sesame, taro pasta, etc.

Alternatively, you can make homemade fillings if you cannot find ready-made paste.

Make the Dough:

The dough makes up the outer skin of the mooncake. This will make 12-14 mooncakes.

Ingredients:

- Medium bowls
- 115 g pastry flour + more for dusting
- 28 g vegetable oil
- 75 g golden g golden syrup
- 2 g lye water
- One egg + 1 tsp. water for egg wash

Directions:

1. Sieve the flour in a medium-sized bowl and keep.
2. In the other bowl, combine the other ingredients and whisk them together. Add all liquids into the flour, then knead 10-15 Times until smooth. Cover with plastic wrap.

Form the Mooncakes:

You can use any fillings to form your mooncakes.

The total weight of the dough and fill in each mooncake should be equal to the mooncake mold. I used 50 g molds so that each mooncake would be 50 g.

1. Create a flattened dough ball, and wrap it around the fillings
2. Starting from the bottom, begin to fold up the disc around the filling, rotate the filling
3. Lightly dust with some flour to avoid sticking the ball and place on a parchment or silicone-lined baking tray.

Molding Your Dough:

1. Form all the balls, set the oven to 355 F/180 C.
2. Lightly dust your mooncake mold with flour.
3. Insert the ball into the mold and turn it onto the baking tray. Press the rod of the mold down until there is resistance, and then lift the mold while continuing. Continue to press the rod to push the mooncake out.

Bake:

1. Spray the mooncakes with a sprinkle of water on the top of the surface to prevent cracking.
2. Bake the mooncakes for 5 minutes.
3. Meanwhile, whisk one egg and 1 tsp. of water to make an egg wash.
4. Once the mooncakes bake for 5 minutes, Take them out of the oven and apply the egg wash. Ensure that it is a thin layer so that the design can still be seen once baked.
5. Continue to bake for 15-20minutes, or until the mooncakes are well browned.

KEY TOOLS

There aren't many extra things for the tools you need to make mooncakes. You can purchase molds and other devices; however, you can start creating your mooncake with only your basic cake baking tools.

- Measuring Cup: Used for baking, I recommend having several cups. The measurements are at the top of the cup. So have a ¼ cup, ½ cup, etc. This will ensure that your measurements are perfect.
- Measuring Spoons: Again, choose to measure spoons that are individual measurements. It is often good to have two different measuring spoon sets, one for dry and one for wet ingredients.

- Mixing Bowls: I always recommend having at least three mixing bowls of various sizes, but it is better if you have more than that, as you will usually use them when baking.
- Cake Pans: It is important to have a wide range of cake pans, but I strongly recommend them for mooncakes 9 x 13-inch round pans. These are the pans you will use more often, but for Mooncakes, make sure you also have rectangular, and other cake pans available.
- Silicone Molds: These are a must-have, but if you are interested in having more than just a round moon cake, it is good to have a few molds available. You can also purchase baking molds if you prefer to bake the cake in your desired shape.
- Parchment Paper: For covering your pans during baking or when you need to chill, the mooncakes and.
- Individual Treat Bags: To wrap your mooncakes up to give them out to people.

These are the important tools you will need to make your mooncakes and. You can purchase different tools to make your kitchen look like a catering school.

HOW TO STORE

1. Like all other ready-to-eat foods, Mooncakes should be stored with lids and positioned in the upper compartment.
2. Keep in a cool, dry, ventilated place.
3. Do not store directly near sunlight or any sources of heat

TIPS AND TRICKS FOR GETTING THE BEST

After making your round mooncake, you can try making assorted shapes. There is a special mold you can use for this purpose. Be creative at this part because there are lots of fun ideas you can do with your mooncake and when making your Golden Syrup, make sure the granulated sugar you use is recommended.

Always remember not to freeze the white snow mooncakes for too long.

If you are having difficulty making mooncakes at hand, there are cake makers you can buy at many stores, both online and offline.

Mooncakes are popular Chinese delicacies. They are delicious and a delight to look at, but more delightful when creative with your designs. When making mooncakes, always make sure you are having fun because your mood will affect the final results, and make sure all the tools and ingredients you will need are ready. You can watch many video tutorials to learn how to decorate beautiful mooncakes.

CHAPTER 1: SWEET MOONCAKES RECIPES

1. FRUITS MOONCAKES

Preparation Time: 1 hr

Cooking Time: 52 mins.

Servings: 9

Ingredients:

- 100 g. cake flour [plus more for dusting]
- 60 g. honey
- 25 g. cooking oil
- 2 g. alkaline water
- ⅛ tsp. salt
- 30 g. almond
- 30 g. pumpkin seeds
- 25 g. candied winter melon
- 20 g. honey
- 15 ml. sesame oil or regular oil
- 5 g. sugar
- 30 g. glutinous rice flour
- 1 tbsp. water
- One egg yolk
- 1 tbsp. water

- Pinch of salt

Directions:

- Combine hot water, honey, alkaline water, and oil until
- Sieve the flour, add salt, and mix until combined.
- keep for 1hr minimum

For the Filling:

- Keep the temperature at 180 C. Chop all the dried fruits into fine pieces.
- Combine all paste ingredients in a large bowl for the paste.
- Add the chopped dried fruits and seeds and mix
- Divide one dough into two, flatten them, and keep the filling at the center.
- Gently close the gap between the doughs around the filling and roll into a round, smooth ball.
- After baking for 8 minutes, beat the egg yolk with a small pinch of salt and water. Use a brush with soft bristles.
- Return the baking sheet into the oven, the same position, and bake for another 5-8 minutes until your mooncake is golden brown.
- Enjoy with hot tea!

JELLY MOONCAKES

Preparation Time: 30 mins.

Cooking Time: 20 mins.

Servings: 6

Ingredients:

- 40 g. soaked until plumed up
- 800 ml. water
- 3 tsp. salt
- 220 g. caster sugar
- 10 g. corn-flour
- 70 g. evaporated milk
- 2 ½ tbsp. agar-agar powder
- 3 pandan leaves, shredded and knotted
- 100 ml. thick coconut milk
- 2 tbsp. whipping cream
- 1-2 drops violet coloring

- 2 tbsp. chia seeds, soaked

Directions:

For the Fillings:

- Bring the water to a boil and add soaked sago. Cook until it becomes transparent.
- Rinse and strain sago with excess water to remove the starch—dry well.
- Mix water, corn flour, sugar, agar-agar powder, and salt in a pot. Stir and cook over medium-low heat till it boils. Mix sago and evaporated milk, and continue to cook for 20-30 sec.
- Pour mixture into plastic molds watch to solidify.
- Keep in the refrigerator to cool and solidify.
- Remove filling from the mold.
- Prepare the skin by placing water, pandan leaves, sugar, agar-agar powder, and salt in a clean pot. Cook over medium-low heat until it boils.
- Add coconut milk, whipping cream, and coloring. Stir well and continue to cook for 1min and watch the mixture till it's thick. Discard the pandan leaves and remove the pot from heat. Mix in the soaked chia leaves.
- Add a tbsp. of agar-agar mixture into a wet plastic jelly mooncake mold. Set aside for 1-2 mins.
- Keep the filling in the center of the mold and add more agar-agar mixture to fill the mold. Keep it cool, and then place it in the refrigerator to chill and harden completely.

CHOCOLATE MOONCAKES

Preparation Time: 20 mins.

Cooking Time: 40 mins.

Servings: 8

Ingredients:

- 1 box vanilla cake mix box
- ⅔ c. + 3 tbsp. almond milk
- ¼ c. canola oil
- 3 eggs
- ¼ tsp. almond extract
- ½ tsp. vanilla extract
- 1 tsp. green food coloring
- 8 oz. cream cheese frosting
- 2 c. cocoa candy melts

Directions:

- In a bowl, combine cake mix, eggs, almond milk, canola oil, almond extract, vanilla extract, and food coloring until smooth, fold in pistachios.
- Bake cake batter according to cake mix instructions.
- After, let the cake cool completely and then crumble into fine bits in a bowl.
- Stir in cream cheese frosting until dough forms.
- Mold cake dough into tablespoon-size balls and place on a greaseproof paper-lined cookie sheet; chill for at least 1 hour.
- After 1 hour, add candy melts to a bowl and melt in microwave for 30 seconds each, stirring at 10-second intervals until smooth.
- Roll cake balls in candy melt and garnish with more pistachios.
- Let stand to set and enjoy after.

MIXED NUTS MOONCAKE

Preparation Time: 20 mins.

Cooking Time: 50 mins.

Servings: 24

Ingredients:

- Mooncake wrapper
- 230 g. all-purpose flour
- 56 g. peanut oil
- 150 g. golden syrup
- 4 g. lye water
- 1 tbsp. all-purpose flour for coating
- 400 g. mixed nuts and dried fruits
- 25 g. Sugar
- 80 g. Walton
- 5 tbsp. Water
- 70 g. Vegetable oil
- 1 tbsp. Chinese white spirit

- ½ c. glutinous flour
- ½ c. cake flour
- Egg wash
- One egg yolk

Directions:

- Put lye water, golden syrup, and Vegetable oil in a small bowl until well combined and mixed with flour. Stir, Wrap, and then knead several Times to become smooth.
- Keep in the fridge for 2-3 hours.
- Portion out and then divide into 24 equal balls
- Combine glutinous and cake flour and bake for 15 minutes at 180°C.
- Stir twice. Or pan-fry it under low heat until the color turns yellow.
- Melt maltose with water over a slow fire.
- Mix in a nut, sugary flour, white spirit.
- Pour in the syrup.
- Mix well and then fridge until slightly hardened.
- Divide the filling into 30g to 32g balls.
- Take one portion of the wrapper, press it into a round wrapper, and place one filling ball in the center.
- Push the wrapper from bottom to top gently to seal the ball completely.
- Firstly, shape it into a ball and then an oval shape.
- Dust the mooncake tool slightly and press the rod and gently remove the cake from the tool.
- Preset the oven to 180C.
- Spray a very tiny layer of water on the surface to avoid cracking surface (especially you used a larger amount of dusting flour)
- Bake at 180°C for 5 mins.
- Stir the egg yolk and In a small bowl, combine it with egg whites—transfer mooncakes and brush a very thin layer of egg wash on the surface.
- Whisk the egg yolk and combine it with egg whites—transfer mooncakes and brush a very thin layer of egg wash on the surface.
- Continue to bake for around 12 to 15 minutes until the mooncake becomes well browned
- Enjoy your mixed nut with chilled milk or juice.

RED BEAN MOONCAKES

Preparation Time: 20 mins.

Cooking Time: 40 mins.

Servings: 15

Ingredients:

- 2 ½ c. all-purpose flour
- ½ c. canola or other neutral-flavored oil
- ½ c. golden syrup
- 1 tsp. regular or alkaline water (the alkaline water will impart a deeper golden color)
- ¾ c. red bean paste
- 1 large egg
- 2 tbsp. water
- 1 c. dried Asian or adzuki red beans, rinsed and picked over
- ½ c. sugar
- ½ c. canola oil
- More all-flour for dusting

Directions:

For Dough Preparation:

- Combine flour, alkaline water, golden syrup, and canola oil.
- Mix to form a shaggy dough. Using a flexible spatula, knead with your hands to create a smooth and cohesive dough.
- Create the dough into a thick disc, wrap it
- Allow it to rest for 45 minutes at room temperature
- Preheat the oven to 350°C and arrange a large, rimmed baking sheet with parchment paper.
- Share the dough into 12 equal parts with a bench scraper (weigh with a digital scale).
- Form a smooth ball from each piece
- Form a piece of a smooth ball
- Work piece of dough at a Time, flatten with your palm and form into a 4-inch size.
- Dust with flour if sticking. Use a bench scraper to help lift the dough. Fill with ½ tbsp. bean paste.
- Top with additional paste ½ tbsp.
- Adjust until it completely wraps the filling and rolls into a smooth ball.
- Set the balls on the baking sheet already prepared, spacing at least 2 inches apart. Lightly dust the mooncake mold with flour. Press the plunger of the mold down to apply pressure but take care not to press too hard. Gently release from the mold. Follow the same process for the rested dough and filling to form more
- Observe until it turns golden-yellow in the oven. Baking takes about 10-15 mins
- Take the sheet away from the oven and cool the cakes on the sheet for 10 minutes.
- In a small bowl, prepare the egg wash.

- I am using a pastry brush, coat the mooncakes in egg wash.
- Bake again in the oven until it forms a deep golden-brown color.
- Cool the mooncakes on the sheet.
- Allow 1 to 2 days for the dough to soften before Servings by storing mooncakes in an airtight container at room temperature.

For the Red Paste Fillings:

- Keep 4 inches of water in a large bowl and soak overnight. Remove the water. Wash the beans.
- In a medium saucepan, combine the beans with 2 inches of water.
- Bring the water to a simmer and cook for 40 to 50 minutes, or until the beans are cooked. Drain and rinse the beans under cool water.
- Add the sugar to the beans in the bowl of a food processor. Puree until completely smooth.
- In a medium nonstick skillet, pour the paste. Cook, constantly stirring with a flexible spatula, over medium-low heat until smooth and mixed. In 8 to 10 minutes, add the remaining ¼ c. oil and simmer, constantly stirring, until the color of the paste has deepened, and the oil has been absorbed completely.
- Move paste to a heat-proof container and set aside to cool completely.
- Refrigerate until ready to use. Place the paste in an enclosed container for two weeks or frozen for three months.

TARO COCONUT SNOWY MOONCAKES

Preparation Time: 1 hr.

Cooking Time: 40 mins.

Servings: 10

Ingredients:

- 340 g. Taro
- ⅓ c. Coconut milk, unsweetened full fat
- 180 g. Coconut milk, unsweetened full fat
- ½ c. Granulated sugar
- 45 g. Icing sugar
- ½ tsp. Kosher salt
- 50 g. Rice flour, glutinous
- 35 g. Rice flour
- ¼ c. Rice flour, toasted
- 20 g. Tapioca flour
- 3/16 c. Vegetable oil

- 15 g. Vegetable

Directions:

For the Taro Coconut Filling:

- Wash and peel taro root with a peeler tool. Wear gloves to prevent itchiness.
- Steam Taro until soft (30-40min)
- Remove taro from the steamer.
- Mash the taro into a smooth paste using a fork
- Include salt, vegetable oil, and sugar inside the mixture
- Mix until well combined, and paste turns smooth.
- Add coconut milk to the mixture and mix thoroughly.
- Make the paste consistent by adding coconut milk
- Whisk together glutinous rice flour, tapioca flour, and icing sugar in a separate bowl.
- Combine the wet and dry mixture, mix until there are no lumps
- Strain mixture through a sieve finely meshed.
- Steam the mixture until it becomes slightly transparent (30 minutes).
- Turn the mixture with chopsticks for several minutes after Removing the bowl from the pot until the mixture is glossy and smooth.
- Knead for a few minutes, or until oily. Form the dough into a disc. Keep in the fridge for two hours before assembling the snow skin mooncake. Warm dough is too sticky to handle.
- Keep and cool the filling. Refrigerate the mixture.

For the Snow Skin Mooncake:

- Whisk together glutinous rice flour, tapioca flour, and icing sugar in a separate bowl.
- Mix both wet and dry mixture and ensure that no lumps remain.
- Strain mixture through a sieve.
- Steam the mixture until it becomes slightly transparent (30 minutes).
- Turn the mixture with chopsticks for several minutes after removing the bowl from the pot to make it smooth and glossy.
- Cover dough with saran wrap and place on a plate.
- Knead for a few minutes or until a greasy surface appears.
- Form a disc with the dough and refrigerate for two hours before assembling the snow skin mooncake. Warm dough is too sticky to handle. Weigh 75-g. scoops of taro filling and gently shape each portion into balls. Set aside.
- Share and weigh the dough into eight 35-g. pieces.
- Dust the mooncake mold with toasted rice flour.

- With the aid of a wrapper dough, seal the fillings completely. Shape into an oval shape to easily slide into the mooncake mold. More toasted rice flour should be sprinkled on the mooncake ball's bottom.
- Press on the mooncake mold to shape the mooncake. Carefully remove from the mold. If any sides of the mooncake are too tacky, brush on toasted rice flour.

HONEY PISTACHIO MOONCAKE

Preparation Time: 20 mins.

Cooking Time: 35 mins.

Servings: 10

Ingredients:

- 2 ½ c. all-purpose flour, plus more for dusting
- ½ c. canola or other neutral-flavored oil
- ½ c. golden syrup
- 1 tsp. alkaline water
- ¼ c. of honey
- 2 tbsp. coconut oil
- 1 tbsp. cornstarch
- 1 tsp. coarse salt

For the Egg Wash:

- 1 large egg
- 2 tbsp. water

Directions:

For the Dough:

- Mix golden syrup, flour, canola oil, and alkaline water in a large mixing bowl.
- Continue mixing to form a shaggy dough, then knead with your bare hands to create a smooth and sticky dough.
- Make a thick disc from the dough, wrap it in plastic, and allow it to rest at room temperature for 45 minutes.
- Set the oven temperature and line a large, rimmed baking sheet with parchment paper.

For the Filling:

- Pulse the pistachios until coarsely ground in the food processor bowl. Add cornstarch, honey, coconut oil, salt, and thump more.

- When you press the filling, it should stick together (Do not overdo this step to avoid getting an entirely new product). Portion the fillings into twelve and mold a ball from each
- Work on one ball at a Time, flatten the round ball. Wrap the filling inside the dough and roll it into a smooth ball. Organize them on the baking sheet already prepared and dust slightly. Adjust a bit without pressure and return it to the baking sheet. Bake for close to 11 mins until you observe a golden-brown color. Offload it from the oven and cool for 10 mins. Brush with egg wash using a brush. Return to the oven for final baking for up to 10 min and allow mooncakes to cool completely before Servings.

PLUM BLOSSOM MOONCAKES

Preparation Time: 40 mins.

Cooking Time: 20 mins.

Servings: 20

Ingredients:

- 160 g. all-purpose flour sifted
- 25 g. icing sugar
- 50 g. margarine
- 75 g. water
- 110 g. all-purpose flour
- 70 g. shortening
- 300 g. red bean paste
- 1 egg yolk, lightly beaten
- 2 tbsp. Black Sesame Seeds

Directions:

- Divide red bean paste into 15 g. portions, roll into twenty balls, and keep aside. Make water dough in a mixing container and mix flour, icing sugar, and margarine. Mix and add water.
- Mix into a soft yellow dough and keep for 10 minutes.
- Prepare oil dough into ten portions and form into balls and let the dough rest for 10 minutes.
- Share the dough into two halves by cutting cross-sectionally from the center. Flatten the dough and wrap it up with the red bean paste fillings.
- Brush the top slightly with beaten egg yolk and sprinkle some sesame seeds in the depression.
- Bake in the oven pre-heated at 190°C until it achieved a golden-brown color. Remove from the baking tray from oven to cool on for 5 minutes

LOTUS SEED PASTE MOONCAKES

Preparation Time: 30 mins.

Cooking Time: 40 mins.

Servings: 19

Ingredients:

- 125 g. golden syrup
- 40 g. groundnut oil
- ½ tsp. alkaline water
- 180 g. all-purpose flour
- 450 g. lotus seed paste
- 50 g. melon seeds, toasted
- 30 g. white sesame seeds, toasted
- 1 tbsp. Honey
- ½ tsp. water
- 1 mooncake mold, 50 g.

Directions:

- Preparing the skin dough for the mooncake, you will first mix the groundnut oil, golden syrup, and alkaline water in a separate bowl. Be assured that they are perfectly blended before considering adding flour.
- Work on the flour by folding and mixing it until the sticky dough is formed. Cover and let it relax for four hours. Share into equal portions 15g each
- Toast melon seeds, bake salted egg yolks.
- Make the mooncake filling by toasting melon and white sesame seeds for 5 mins in a set oven at 175°C and cool it
- Mix melon and sesame seeds with lotus paste.
- Once cooled, combine and mix well into lotus seed paste filling. Roll and Cut into pieces.
- Also, roll and cut the lotus seed paste filling
- Wrap filling in the skin.
- Flatten the skin dough and place one filling ball in the center
- Wrap pastry skin around filling and Place the mooncake in the mold to impart your designs and release from the mold then you have your mooncake already. Place mooncakes on a baking tray.
- Place the baking tray in the oven already set at a temperature of 190°C and bakc for 10 mins or until the edges turn golden. Remove and cool for some minutes. Make a honey-water glaze and rub the top of the cake with the glaze,

then carry out a second bake to last for about 5 minutes until you observe a golden-brown color. Then remove and cool completely.
- Transfer the baked mooncakes to cool completely on a wire rack before storing them in an airtight container. Serve alongside hot Chinese tea.

OREO MOONCAKES

Preparation Time: 30 mins.

Cooking Time: 40 mins.

Servings: 16

Ingredients:

- 200 g. Snow skin premix powder (icing sugar and Kou fen)
- 40 g. shortening
- 80 ml. hot water
- 250 g. cream cheese, soft
- 50 g. Oreo biscuits, crushed
- 30 g. icing sugar, sifted

Directions:

- Roll Oreo biscuits in a Ziploc bag to crush. Mix softened cream, icing sugar, and cheese together. Fold in crushed Orco biscuits and chill for about an hour. Make sure the Oreo biscuit is firm enough to handle, portion it into 40d portions each, roll to balls, and keep it in the freezer.
- Using the Snowskin premix powder, add hot water and knead to form a smooth dough, also into 40g portion too
- Dust each portion with some kou fen (fried glutinous rice flour) and roll out thinly
- Wrap the rolled-out snow skin around the Oreo cheese filling and squeeze the bottom edges together to seal.
- Place it in a mooncake mold that has been lightly coated with kou fen and firmly push it in.
- Remove the mooncake from the oven and place it in the refrigerator until ready to serve.

VIETNAMESE MOONCAKES

Preparation Time: 20 mins.

Cooking Time: 50 mins.

Servings: 20

Ingredients:

- 1 c. brown/caster sugar
- ½ c. Water
- 1.25 tsp. Lye water
- ½ tbsp. Lime Juice
- 320 g. All-purpose flour
- 200 g. Sugar Syrup
- 50 ml. vegetable oil
- 150 g. candied lime peel, roughly chopped
- 100 g. candied orange peel, roughly chopped
- 50g. ginger jam
- 150g. Chinese sausages, diced
- 4 tbsp. sesame seeds
- 1 tsp. sesame oil
- 3 tbsp. cooked glutinous rice flour
- 3 tbsp. corn syrup

Directions:

- To make sugar syrup get a little cooking pan, mix sugar and water. Boil, then lower the warmth to simmer.
- Don't stir. Simply shake the pan to assist the sugar dissolving. Then add juice and acidic water.

- You will be able to skim off the foam. Simmer for 10-15 minutes till slightly thickened. To check for thickness, drop the sweetener inside a bowl of cold water. Until it forms little circles, shut down the warmth, and cool and store inside a jar.
- To create the crust, place the general-purpose flour in a bowl. Create a hole within the center and pour oil, lye water, and syrup into the cavity. Stir well till it is combined.
- Knead well together with your hand. Let the dough rest for a half-hour. To create the filling, place the haywire, candied peel, ginger jam inside a pan, and dry-fry on medium-low heat, mix perpetually.
- Add the rice flour and syrup step by step. Add roasted seeds and oil. Turn the mixture till it gets sticky. Ensure every ball weighs ⅔ of the overall weight of the cake.
- To form the cake, divide the dough into equal portions; every portion weighs ⅓ of the overall weight of the cake. Roll every portion flat, place a filling ball within the center, and wrap it up.
- Flour the cake to avoid breaking. Place the formed ball into the middle and press to implement the pattern. Repeat till the end of the dough and fillings.
- Preheat the kitchen appliance Salted Caramel Cake Pops to 175°c/350°. Place the formed mooncake on a bright color. Bake for ten minutes. Then remove, spray water to cool down, and let it dry for ten minutes.
- Prepare the egg wash; combine the ingredients with water and food coloring. Gently tap/brush the egg wash onto the surface of the cakes.
- Bake for an additional 5-10 minutes.
- Freshly baked mooncakes are ready to eat because the crust is firm. Enjoy it with tea or juice.

DURIAN MOONCAKES

Preparation Time: 40 mins.

Cooking Time: 60 mins.

Servings: 20

Ingredients:

- 11 g. gelatin plus
- 2 tbsp. water
- 300 g. fresh or frozen durian pulp
- 125 g. snow skin pinpe flour
- 30 g. GaoFen. cooked/fried glutinous flour)
- 130 g. water/carrot juice
- 25 g. icing sugar
- 1-2 drop coloring
- 25 g. shortening

- 1tbsp. garden, for dusting

Directions:

- Microwave the gelatin with the water for 1 minute or until the gelatin is completely dissolved. Add to the durian pulp. Scoop 25 g of the durian filling and roll into a ball. Wrap tightly with clear food wrap.
- Refrigerate for 30 minutes to an hour.
- Combine the snow skin (pinpe) and GaoFen. Set aside.
- Mix the water or carrot juice with the shortening and icing sugar in a pot.
- Bring to a boil, constantly stirring, using a hand whisk. With a rubber spatula, fold in the hot water mixture until the flour is smooth and a soft dough forms. After adding the color, knead for 1–2 minutes.
- To wrap the durian filling in the dough, dust it with gaofen and divide it into 30 g balls. Gently push the mooncake into the mold to make it a mooncake shape.
- To release the mooncakes, turn the mold over and lightly tap it. Keep the mooncake in an airtight container until ready to serve.
- Chill for many hours, preferably overnight, before serving.

LAVA CUSTARD MOONCAKES

Preparation Time: 20 mins.

Cooking Time: 30 mins.

Servings: 12

Ingredients:

- Flour
- Eggs
- 1 Salted egg yolk
- 15 g. Unsalted butter
- 2 g. Gelatin powder
- 7 g. Custard powder
- 25 g. Icing sugar
- 30 g. Whipping cream
- Chinese rose with a dash
- 30 g. Water
- A pinch of salt

Directions:

- Place the chilled pastry dough on a baking pan. Knead it into a ball, then cut it into 28 g portions. In a Ziplock bag, place the dough.
- With your hand or a rolling pin, flatten it into a circle. Along the rim, the dough should be thinner.
- Wrap the dough around one piece of the custard filling.
- Dust the mooncake with flour before shaping it. Form a cylinder with the dough and place it in the mold. With your hand, gently press.
- Invert the mold. To remove the mooncake, press ten Times.
- One hour after pressing the mooncakes, place them in the refrigerator.
- Preheat the Air fryer for 10 minutes at 200°C. Before placing the mooncakes on the baking tray, spray them with water—Bake for 5 minutes at 200°C.
- Along with the mooncakes, remove the baking tray. The egg wash should be applied in a thin layer. Allow 10 minutes for the mooncakes to come to room temperature.
- Bake after a second egg washing.

ICE-CREAM MOONCAKES

Preparation Time: 40 mins.

Cooking Time: 60 mins.

Servings: 6

Ingredients:

- Mango sherbet and orange sherbet, for the middle portion of the moon
- Vanilla ice cream, for the middle moon section
- Ice cream with strawberries
- 1 pt. coffee ice cream
- 1 c. biscuit, crushed
- 3 tbsp. melted butter
- 2 c. chocolate chips
- ¼ c. coconut oil

Directions:

- Scoop out orange/mango sherbet balls or vanilla ice cream balls using a melon baller or cookie scoop. The moons inside the ice cream mooncake will be these. Freeze for two hours after placing on parchment paper.

- Make the biscuit crumbs while the ice cream balls are freezing. Crust one cup (100g) of Biscuits, add the melted butter, and toss until the crumbs are evenly coated in butter and hold together when packed.
- Place a strawberry or coffee ice cream layer in your ice cream form or cup.
- Using a melon baller or a cookie scoop, place a Preparation ball. Freeze for two hours after placing on parchment paper. Scoop out orange/mango sherbet balls or vanilla ice cream balls. The moons inside the ice cream mooncake will be these.
- Make the biscuit crumbs while the ice cream balls are freezing. 1 c. (100g) biscuits, melted butter, and whisk.

PINEAPPLE FILLED GLUTEN-FREE MOONCAKES

Preparation Time: 40 mins.

Cooking Time: 25 mins.

Servings: 10

Ingredients:

- 350 g. pineapple, cubed
- 3 tbsp. cornstarch
- 3 tbsp. erythritol or organic raw cane sugar
- 4 tbsp. Vegan butter
- ½ tbsp. coconut oil
- Snow skin
- ⅓ c. glutinous rice flour, traditional watermill
- 2½ tbsp. Cornstarch
- ¼ c. rice flour
- ¼ tsp. pure stevia extract powder
- 4 tsp. Canola oil
- ¾ c. non-dairy milk
- ½ tsp. beet juice concentrate or other natural red dye

Directions:

- In a high-powered blender, combine the diced pineapple, cornstarch, and erythritol, blending until smooth.
- Over medium heat, heat a sauté pan. Add the vegan butter and coconut oil when the sauté pan is hot. Add the pineapple puree and mix well. Cook, covered, for about 25 minutes over medium-low heat. The puree's volume should be reduced to at least half of before.
- To keep the pineapple from burning, stir regularly with a spatula.
- The oil from the pineapple should separate, and the pineapple filling should be sticky at the end.

- The pineapple filling yields roughly 200 g.
- Fill a heatproof bowl halfway with the filling. Refrigerate for at least 2 hours or until completely cooled.

CLASSIC MANGO MOCHI

Preparation Time: 50 mins.

Cooking Time: 20 mins.

Servings: 10

Ingredients:

- Glutinous rice flour
- 1 Fresh mango
- Sugar
- Cornstarch
- Milk
- Coconut milk
- Butter
- Shredded coconut

Directions:

- Add glutinous rice, cornstarch, sugar, milk, coconut milk, and melted butter in a large mixing bowl. Mix until everything is dissolved completely
- Transfer the mixture into a smaller bowl that fits into your steamer.
- Place the bowl into the steamer. Cover with plastic wrap and steam for 10 minutes, or until the dough is slightly transparent. While waiting, cut the mango into small square cubes (about ½ inch)
- Take around 12 spoonfuls of dough and wet your hands with water. Form the dough into a ball and flatten it into a circular shape using your hands.
- Place a piece of mango in the water. Pinch the four corners of the mocha wrapper, and then pinch the remaining corners together.
- Coat the mocha ball with shredded coconut. Chill the mango mocha balls in the refrigerator for 30 minutes before serving.

PLUM BLOSSOM MOONCAKE

Preparation Time: 35 mins.

Cooking Time: 50 mins.

Servings: 16

Ingredients:

- 210 g. plain flour
- 20 g. icing sugar
- 200 g. shortening
- 110 ml. water
- 200 g. plain flour
- 720 g. Osmanthus oolong paste
- 80 g. toasted melon seeds
- 1 egg yolk
- 1 tsp. water for egg wash

Directions:

- Divide the filling into 50 g portions. Set aside
- Knead the water and oil doughs into a soft dough, cover, and set aside for 30 minutes. Each component should be cut into 16 pieces.
- Flatten the water dough and wrap it in a portion of oil dough—seal edge and shape round. Flatten into an oval shape and roll up like a Swiss roll. Turn the roll, flatten, and roll up like a Swiss roll again. Wrap it with a portion of the filling and seal the edge firmly and shape round.
- Cut into a plum blossom flower shape. Glaze it with egg yolk and bake in a preheated oven at 180°C for 20-25 minutes until golden brown.
- Cool completely before storing.

APPLE SHAPED STEAMED BUNS MOONCAKE

Preparation Time: 25 mins.

Cooking Time: 10 mins.

Servings: 8

Ingredients:

- 200 g. all-purpose flour
- 40 g. wheat starch or use cornstarch
- 3 g. instant yeast
- 20 g. granulated sugar
- 1 tbsp. Cooking oil
- ¼ tsp. salt
- 120 ml. cold milk, preferably whole full cream milk more as needed
- Red yeast rice powder to color the dough
- 1 tsp. Matcha powder
- ¼ tsp. cocoa powder

For Apple Fillings:

- 500 g. apples, peeled
- 40 g. coconut sugar or more
- 20 g. granulated sugar
- ½ tsp. ground cinnamon
- 1 tbsp. lemon juice
- 120 ml. apple juice or water
- ½ tsp. Salt
- ½ g. vanilla extract
- 10 g. coconut oil
- 1 tbsp. cornstarch
- 2 tbsp. water

Directions:

For the Apple Pie Fillings:

- Prepare the dough by combining the starch, instant yeast, sugar, salt, oil, and mixing bowl. Add 1tbsp. cold milk
- Keep the Colored (red and green) for 10 minutes and cover
- Cut off about 10 g. of green dough. Flatten with the dough and wrap with the fillings
- Shape the buns and mist lightly with water. Proof and steam at moderate temperature for about 8–10 minutes and turn off the heat, leave in the steamer for about 1-2 minutes and remove to cool.
- Serve while warm.

BUTTERFLY PEA MOONCAKE

Preparation Time: 27 mins.

Cooking Time: 14 mins.

Servings: 4

Ingredients:

- 400 ml. warm water to extract blue pea flower
- 1 tbsp. blue pea flower
- 120 g. sugar
- 100 ml. coconut cream
- 4 g. agar-agar powder

Directions:

- Make dough according to the dough recipe.
- Mix all ingredients and stir until it is blended. Put it in a saucepan and allow it to boil.
- Allow 5 minutes for the dried pea blossoms to soak in warm water. Squeeze out excess liquid from the flower, and you will get blue color water. Discard the flowers and make use of the water.
- Pour into the mold and allow it to rest for 2-3 minutes.

CHRYSANTHEMUM MOONCAKES

Preparation Time: 1hr. 30 mins.

Cooking Time: 30 mins.

Servings: 9

Ingredients:

- One portion of mung bean
- 8 passion fruits
- 120 g. all-purpose flour
- ¼ tsp. turmeric powder
- 80 g. sugar syrup
- 7 g. cooking oil
- ½ egg yolk, gently beaten
- 5 g. peanut butter
- Zest of 1 lemon
- ½ egg yolk + egg white for egg wash
- 1 tsp. water

Directions:

- Make dough according to dough mix instructions
- Make a batter with all the ingredients and steam it until it hardens to make the skin. Then knead briefly into a dough. Add all the ingredients for the fillings into a saucepan.
- Divide the dough and the fillings into equal pieces. Wrap the ingredients in the dough and roll it into a ball. Bake for 20 minutes, then cool and serve.

CHAPTER 2: EASY MOONCAKES RECIPES

HAM MOONCAKES

Preparation Time: 25 mins.

Cooking Time: 20 mins.

Servings: 20

Ingredients:

- 250 g. of ham (Xuan Wei ham or prosciutto ham preferred)
- 150 g. of plain flour
- 2 g. of dried rose petals
- 2 g. of salt
- 60 g. of honey
- 50 g. of lard or cooking oil

Directions:

- Pour the cooked flour into the ham-filling.
- Share mooncake into 9g each.
- Use the rolling pin to press flat and put the fillings and wrap.
- Dust the mooncake mold with flour.
- Set in the mooncake. Remove the shaped mooncake.
- Put the mooncake in the baking tray and bake for about 5 minutes.
- Take it out, brush and bake for another 10-15 minutes.
- The cake is ready. When the surface is golden brown.

BLUE PEA FLOWER MOONCAKES

Preparation Time: 2 hrs. 10 mins.

Cooking Time: 28 mins.

Servings: 20

Ingredients:

- 20 blue pea flowers + 80ml. water
- 35 g. glutinous rice flour
- 30 g. rice flour
- 20 g. wheat starch (or cornstarch)
- 30 g. icing sugar, sifted
- 125 ml. blue pea flower water (50ml.) + milk (75ml.)
- 35 g. corn oil
- 250 g. red dragon lotus paste – 25 g. each (10 pcs)
- Some kao fen (cooked glutinous rice flour) for dusting

Directions:

- For a minute, boil 20 blue pea blossoms + 80ml water with one pandan leaf. Cover and set aside to cool, then filter to obtain 50ml blue pea flower water.
- Blend all dry ingredients in a mixing dish and thoroughly combine them. Stir in the milk with the blue pea flowers thoroughly. After that, add the corn oil and completely combine everything.
- In a buttered (cooking oil) baking dish, strain the mixture. Prick several holes with a skewer and cover the baking dish with aluminum foil.
- Cook on high heat for 25 minutes. After steaming, the baked dough will have a film of oil on top of it.

- Cut the dough into rough shapes using a rubber spatula and knead it together in a plastic bag. When it's not too hot to handle, knead it by hand into a smooth dough. Refrigerate it after wrapping it with cling wrap.

MINI LOTUS MOONCAKES

Preparation Time: 2 hrs.

Cooking Time: 20 mins.

Servings: 20

Ingredients:

- 300 g. dried lotus seeds, makes about 800 g. lotus seed paste
- ½ tbsp. alkaline water
- 250 g. sugar
- 200 g. vegetable oil
- 30 g. maltose
- 190 g. golden syrup
- 50 g. groundnut oil
- 1 tsp. alkaline water
- 250 g. all-purpose flour
- 600 g. lotus seed paste
- 60 g. melon seeds, toasted
- 1 egg yolk, lightly beaten
- 1 mooncake mold

Directions:

- Combine all ingredients in a batter and steam to solidify to make the skin. Then knead for a few minutes to make a dough.
- In a saucepan, combine all the ingredients for the filling. Heat it in a hot water bath until it solidifies.
- Cut the dough and contents into equal-sized pieces. To create a ball, wrap the filling in the dough.

SNOW SKIN CUSTARD MOONCAKES

Preparation Time: 1 hr. 30 mins.

Cooking Time: 25 mins.

Servings: 12

Ingredients:

- 3 tbsp. glutinous rice flour
- 3 tbsp. rice flour
- 2 tbsp. wheat starch (or cornstarch)
- 3 tbsp. icing sugar sifted
- ½ c. milk
- 1 tbsp. condensed milk
- 1 tbsp. cooking oil
- 45 g. unsalted butter, melted
- 2 eggs, lightly beaten
- 2½ tbsp. wheat starch (or cornstarch)
- ½ c. powdered milk (or two tbsp. condensed milk)
- 3 tbsp. icing sugar sifted

Directions:

- All the components for the skin should be whisked together in a mixing dish. Fill a deep plate halfway with the mix.
- Cook for 15 minutes over medium heat in a steamer with the plate. Increase the steaming Time by 5 minutes if you double the recipe.
- Remove the hardened dough from the platter using a spatula. Knead with hands (using gloves to avoid sticking) until smooth and elastic once cold enough to touch. Refrigerate for at least two hours before Servings (covered). Fill the dough in equal portions after dividing it (a kitchen scale helps). Make balls with the filling.
- With your hands, flatten a dough piece. It should be wrapped around a filler component. Gently press the wrapper upwards to thoroughly seal the filling (be careful not to leave any room or air between the skin and the filling).

MINCED PORK MEAT MOONCAKES

Preparation Time: 25 mins

Cooking Time: 20 mins

Servings: 18

Ingredients:

- 1 egg, lightly whisked
- 1 tbsp. sesame seeds
- Mayonnaise, to serve

- ¾ c. plain flour
- 80 g. lard, melted
- 1 ½ c. plain flour
- 1 ½ tbsp. caster sugar
- 40 g. lard, melted
- ¼ c. cold water
- 250 g. pork minced
- 3 cm-piece fresh ginger, peeled, finely grated
- 2 garlic cloves, crushed
- 2 green shallots, thinly sliced
- 1 tbsp. Chinese cooking wine

Directions:

- To prepare the lard dough, knead the flour and lard together in a mixing bowl until a smooth dough forms. After covering in plastic wrap, chill for 30 minutes.
- Combine the flour, sugar, and lard for the water dough in a mixing bowl. Mix in 60ml (¼ c.) water with a flat-bladed knife to produce a soft dough, adding more water if necessary. It is unacceptable if the dough is dry. Wrap the dish in plastic wrap and set it aside. Combine all ingredients and season with salt and pepper to fill in a mixing dish. On a dish, make 12 even balls. Refrigerate until ready to use.
- Divide the water dough into 12 equal parts with your hands and knead each ball until smooth.
- Cover with a damp paper towel. Repeat with the lard dough. Take one portion of water dough and flatten it into a 10cm disc. Place a lard dough portion in the center and pull up the sides to enclose the lard dough. Roll out the combined dough on a lightly floured surface to form an oval about 15-20cm in length. Roll into a log shape, then turn 90 degrees. Use a rolling pin to roll out to form a long rectangular strip. Roll up. Roll up tightly into a log shape. Stand upright on a plate. Cover. Repeat to create 12 logs of dough.
- Preheat oven to 190°C/170°C fan forced. Grease and line a large baking tray. Flatten a pastry log and roll out on a lightly floured surface into a 10cm disc. Place a pork ball in the middle. Use your fingers to fold up the sides to enclose the filling and seal the base. Place, sealed side down, on the prepared tray and flatten slightly. Repeat with remaining pastry and filling.

WHITE LOTUS MOONCAKES

Preparation Time: 40 mins.

Cooking Time: 20 mins.

Servings: 9

Ingredients:

- 125 g. Invert syrup
- 4 g. Jianshui
- 40 g. Peanut oil
- 115 g. High-gluten flour
- 50 g. All-purpose flour
- 1 g. salt
- 1 egg
- 1 bag (500 g.) White lotus paste filling
- 1 bag (20 pcs) yolk

Directions:

- Soak the egg yolk with brown wine (5 minutes is fine) or pour the brown wine into a small watering can, place the egg yolk on a baking tray lined with greased paper, and spray the brown wine 2-3 times.
- Put the egg yolks into the oven at 150°C for 8-10 minutes. Be careful not to crack the egg yolk. Now you can prepare the mooncake crust. Mix the inverted syrup with liquid water and mix well.
- Pour in peanut oil and stir well. Sift the flour, add a small amount of sifted flour, mix well, and pour the remaining flour on the panel.
- Weigh 40 g. of white lotus seed paste, press flat, and place egg yolks for later use. Weigh 25 g. of mooncake skin and roll it into rounds for later use. If the room is dry, you can cover it with plastic wrap to prevent the skin and stuffing from drying out.
- Pour the mixed butter into the panel and mix well with the remaining flour until there is no dry powder. Wrap in nylon and put inside the refrigerator for 30 minutes – 1 hour.

MINI SNOW SKIN MOONCAKES

Preparation Time: 30 mins.

Cooking Time: 30 mins.

Servings: 17

Ingredients:

- 60 g. powdered sugar
- 215 g. whole milk
- 25 g. vegetable oil
- 50 g. glutinous sweet rice flour
- 35 g. wheat starch

Directions:

- Combine all ingredients in a batter and steam until firm to make the skin. Then knead for a few minutes to form a dough.
- In a saucepan, combine all the filling ingredients. Heat it in a hot water bath until it becomes a solid mass.
- Make equal portions of the dough and fill. To make a ball, wrap the filling in the dough.

SALTED EGG YOLK MOONCAKE

Preparation Time: 25 mins.

Cooking Time: 40 mins.

Servings: 2

Ingredients:

- 5 salted duck egg yolks
- 2 tbsp. sugar syrup
- ⅓ c. peanut oil or corn oil
- 1 tsp. lye water
- 1 ¾ c. flour (plus more for dusting)

Directions:

- Roll the lotus paste into a long strip and portion it into small pieces
- Flatten the lotus paste, and wrap It around the salty egg yolk
- Position the lotus paste on a pastry skin
- Wrap the lotus paste into the pastry skin and form a pastry from it
- Brush it with egg wash
- Place in a baking pan
- Bake for 25 minutes in a pre-set oven
- Remove the Pastry from the heat and serve hot

CHICKEN FLOSS MOONCAKE

Preparation Time: 20 mins.

Cooking Time: 40 mins.

Servings: 18

Ingredients:

- 150 g. bread flour
- 110 g. all-purpose flour
- 4 tbsp. sugar
- 100 g. cold butter, chopped
- 90 ml. water
- 150 g. all-purpose flour
- 100 g. shortening
- Egg glazing: 1 egg yolk + 1 tsp. milk
- ½ c. sesame seeds

Directions:

- Add all ingredients (except water) to a large mixing bowl and knead the butter and dry ingredients until thoroughly incorporated.
- Then, add enough water to produce a soft, non-stick dough.
- Kneading till smooth, then set aside. Combine all ingredients in a large mixing bowl, divide them into 14 sections, wrap them in the dough, and bind them together to form a ball. Allow for a rest period of 20 minutes. Please see here for further information on different rolling methods. Roll the pastry dough into a spherical shape to flatten it after pressing both ends into the center.
- Fill with one spoonful of chicken floss, top with a piece of mochi, then seal with 50 g. pandan do yong, place the sealing part down, transfer the filled dough to a baking dish coated with parchment paper, brush with egg glaze, and sprinkle with sesame seeds.

CREAM CHEESE MOONCAKE

Preparation Time: 30 mins.

Cooking Time: 50 mins.

Servings: 10

Ingredients:

- 200 g. Snow Skin Mix
- 50 g. Anchor UHT Full Cream Milk
- 80 g. Cold Water
- 20 g. Shortening
- Koh Fun (dusting)
- 150 g. Anchor Cream Cheese
- 150 g. White Lotus Paste
- 15 g. Raspberry Jam
- 45 g. Koh Fun
- 1 g. Red coloring

Directions:

- Mix the snow skin mix with cold water, Anchor UHT Full Cream Milk, and Raspberry Jam to make the snow skin.
- Mix until everything is well combined, then massage in the shortening.
- Allow cooling before making the raspberry cream cheese filling.
- Anchor Cream Cheese should be softened in a mixing basin. Add the white lotus paste and divide the snow skin dough into 30 g portions.
- Place the filling in the middle of the snow skin dough and roll it out flat.
- Pinch the ends together and have fun!

FISH DOLL MOONCAKE

Preparation Time: 25 mins

Cooking Time: 20 mins

Servings: 18

Ingredients:

- Golden Syrup
- Peanut Oil
- ½ tbsp. Alkaline Water
- 1 tbsp. All-Purpose Flour
- 4 ⅓ c. All-Purpose Flour
- 3 ½ tbsp. Melon Seeds
- 3 tbsp. White Sesame Seeds

- ¼ c. Walnuts
- 2 ¾ c. Chicken Floss or Dried Shredded Chicken
- 1 Egg, yolk only
- 1 tbsp. Water

Directions:

- Pour the golden syrup into a bowl. Measure peanut oil into a bowl.
- Pour the oil into the golden syrup. Add 1 tbsp. Alkaline water.
- Add 2 tbsp. All-purpose flour and stir until well combined. Cover and set aside overnight.
- Mix in a different flour, roasted melon seeds, and white sesame. Pour in the golden syrup mixture and mix.
- Mix until well combined for a soft dough. Do not knead. Cover and allow to rest for 2 hours. Prepare chicken floss Na a fished-shaped mooncake. Dust well, shape the dough into a ball. Fill the center of each dough with some chicken floss.
- Measure 300g peanut oil into a bowl. Press the dough into the mooncake mold.
- Arrange a baking tray in a 190°C preheated oven for 10 minutes. Remove from oven and allow to cool for 15 minutes.
- Bake again for 8 minutes and achieve a golden-brown color. You can wait for up to 1 or 2 days before serving.

COFFEE SNOW SKIN MOONCAKES

Preparation Time: 30 mins

Cooking Time: 5 mins

Servings: 15

Ingredients:

- 25 g. Kao fen
- 115 g. Snow skin flour (KCT pinpe premix powder)
- 25 g. icing sugar
- 23 g. Crisco
- 150 g. Water
- 2 tsp. Coffee powder
- ½ tbsp. Kahlua liqueur
- 1 tbsp. Coffee paste or Chocolate paste
- More Kao for dusting

- 375 Coffee lotus paste, divided into 15 portions, 25g each

Directions:

- Mix the Kao fen and the snow skin flour in a medium bowl and keep aside.
- Add icing sugar, Crisco, and water in a container, then boil the mixture. Stir until the Crisco melts, off heat. Add 2 tsp. instant coffee powder, stir well, and finally add ½ tbsp. Kahlua liqueur to it.
- Spout hot liquid mixture to the flour and use a rubber spatula to stir the mixture to a soft dough, adding 1tbsp. coffee paste, mix thoroughly, and leave the ready dough to cool. Knead the dough until it becomes smooth and add a little Kao fen if the dough is sticky.
- Divide the dough into 15 separate portions, each of 20g. Wrap dough around the coffee lotus pastes to shape it into a ball shape.
- Apply some dust of Kao fen and press firmly into the mold. After unmolding it and store it in an airtight container.
- Snow skin mooncakes can be chilled before consumption.

TIRAMISU LOTUS PASTE MOONCAKES

Preparation Time: 12 hrs.

Cooking Time: 2 hrs.

Servings: 18

Ingredients:

- 50 g. Kao fen
- 65 g. icing sugar
- 13 g. shortening
- 40 ml. cold water
- 10 ml. hot water
- 8 g. 3 in 1 coffee mix

Directions:

- Dilute coffee mix with hot water and set aside to cool. Sift Kao fen and Icing Sugar together and mix well.
- Mix in shortening to the Kao fen mixture. Mix cold water and coffee.
- Slowly add the liquid mixture to the dry mix and use a spatula to combine.
- Wrap the dough in clingwrap or put it inside a plastic bag and leave the dough in the fridge to rest for at least 30 mins.
- Weigh the dough according to the mooncake size and wrap the lotus paste filling in.

CHOCOLATE CHIP MOONCAKE

Preparation Time: 3 hrs.

Cooking Time: 20 mins.

Servings: 28

Ingredients:

- 5 c. cake flour, plus more for rolling
- 3 tbsp. custard powder
- 1 ⅔ c. honey
- ¼ c. + 1 tbsp. un-sulphured molasses (not blackstrap)
- 1 tsp. kosher salt
- ¼ c. water
- 1 ½ tsp. baking soda
- ¾ c. + 1 tbsp. peanut oil
- 3 lb. lotus seed paste
- 1 lb. almond paste
- 3 tbsp. vegetable oil
- 2 tsp. kosher salt
- Finely grated zest of 4 oranges
- ⅔ c. dried apricot, finely diced
- ½ c. dried cherries or cranberries
- ½ c. candied ginger, finely diced
- 1 c. toasted almonds, finely chopped
- ½ c. toasted pecans, finely chopped
- 5 oz. high-quality dark chocolate, roughly chopped
- 5 oz. high-quality milk chocolate, roughly chopped
- 1 large egg, beaten with 1 tbsp. water, for egg wash

Directions:

- Mix the flour with the custard powder in a bowl. Combine the honey, molasses, and salt in a high-sided saucepan and boil. Also, stir a mixture of baking soda with ¼ c. of water in a separate bowl.
- Add the baking soda and cook to the boiling syrup, then stir for 3 seconds to make the syrup bubble up. Stop the heat and pour the peanut oil and the flour into the mixer at medium speed. Mix the dough until it becomes smooth for 90 seconds. And then change into a ball and wrap the plastic up. Leave the dough at room temperature for a minimum of two hours.

- Share the dough into 2-oz. balls and position it on a parchment paper-lined baking sheet. Wrap up the baking sheet in plastic and observe it at room temperature until it is usable. If you are making the dough ahead, keep it in the refrigerator to meet the room temperature standard before proceeding.

- Keep the oven at a temperature of 375°. Beat the lotus seed paste and almond paste, oil, salt, and grind on medium high-speed until it becomes very smooth, all in a bowl of a standing paddle-fitted mixer. Lower the mixer speed and add apricots, cherries and ginger, almonds, and pecans, respectively. Add the chocolates and beat them all together until it was fully blended. Then share the fillings into twenty-eight 3 ½ oz.

- Pieces roll each of the pieces into a ball.

- Using a rolling pin, flatten each dough ball into a circle. Place a ball of filling in the centre of each dough, wrap the dough around the filling, smooth up the surface, and repeat. Place each dough-wrapped ball into a mooncake paddle's lightly dusted cavity and press to fill the mould. Bang the mooncake paddle on a work surface on either side to loosen the mooncake, then turn the paddle over so the cavity is facing down and bang the paddle to release the mooncake, which will fall onto the work surface. Spray liberally with water and place the moulded mooncakes on parchment paper-lined baking trays, spacing them 2 inches apart.

- The mooncakes bake in only about ten minutes, after which they should be taken out of the oven and rubbed with egg wash. Keep the oven temperature at 350° and bake till it colours, changes to Golden-brown, and warms in the centre. This will take about the first 5 minutes more. Finally, bring out the mooncakes from the oven and transfer them to a rack for cooling purposes. Naturally, it is a good practice to allow the mooncake to remain under room temperature sealed in an air-tight container.

STRAWBERRY SNOW SKIN MOONCAKES

Preparation Time: 60 mins.

Cooking Time: 30 mins.

Servings: 5

Ingredients:

- ⅓ c. Glutinous rice flour
- ⅓ c. rice flour
- 2 tbsp. wheat corn starch
- 1 tbsp. white sugar
- 2 tbsp. Milk
- 1 vegetable coloring
- 2 tsp. Milk powder
- 3 tbsp. Cornstarch
- 4 tsp. Milk

- 2 Eggs
- ¼ c. sugar
- 2 tsp. Unsalted butter
- 2 tbsp. Glutinous rice flour for dusting
- 5 small strawberries

Directions:

- Whisk the milk powder, cornstarch, milk, egg, and sugar in a mixing dish.
- Stir the custard base constantly until it thickens in a small saucepan over medium heat.
- Using a rubber spatula, continue mixing the custard until it thickens enough to form balls. Stop the heat and add the butter
- Add the butter until it fully blends
- Wrap the custard in the clingwrap and place it in the refrigerator for complete cooling
- Combine the rice flour, wheat/corn starch, white sugar, and milk and whisk together until it becomes smooth
- Enclose the mixture for about 20min until it fully sets at the center.
- Stop the heat and add oil
- Shake the mixture and allow it cool
- Knead the dough manually and observe that the oil is completely absorbed.
- Divide the dough into three equal parts and knead to your satisfaction with the flavor/ color of your desire. Raspberry powder was used in this case
- When the custard cools, divide it into five equal portions and wrap a whole strawberry in each potion to form a ball.
- Coat a ball of the snow skin in the glutinous rice flour and dust the mooncake mold
- Flatten the ball with a rolling pin from a circle.
- Place a custard ball in the center and pull the sides of the snow skin to the enclosed custard.
- Shape the smooth surface of the dough into a mooncake using the already dusted mold
- Keep in the fridge for 1-2 hours set before serving.

CRYSTAL FLOWER MOONCAKE

Preparation Time: 30 mins.

Cooking Time: 10 mins.

Servings: 8

Ingredients:

- 240 g. roasted glutinous rice flour sieved
- 120 g. icing sugar sieved

- 170 g. shortening
- 100 ml. ice water
- 15 g. mixed quinoa
- 30 ml. water
- 150 g. lotus paste
- 1 tbsp. cocoa powder
- 110 g. dates, chopped
- 1 tbsp. brandy
- 60 g. Oreos, chopped roughly
- 30 g. orange peel
- 80 g. pomegranate seeds
- 1 lemon
- I box edible flowers
- Roasted glutinous rice flour

Directions:

- Sieve the flour and icing sugar into one mixing bowl and mix. Add shortening and mixture, beat slowly, and constantly add cold water until the dough binds.
- Add the quinoa and water to a pot and boil until the quinoa cooks. Add the quinoa and other ingredients except for the lemon zest and beat until blended.
- Wrap a portion of the dough around the filling, separate the flower
- Dust some flour onto the mooncake and mold. Remove the mooncake from the dough and chill in the fridge for 5 minutes before serving.

COFFEE SNOW SKIN CHOCOLATE MOONCAKE

Preparation Time: 30 mins.

Cooking Time: 5 mins.

Servings: 15

Ingredients:

- 25 g. Kao fen
- 115 g. Snow skin flour (KCT pipe premix powder)
- 25 g. icing sugar
- 23 g. Crisco
- 150 g. water

- 2 tsp. coffee powder
- 1 ½ tbsp. Kahlua liqueur
- 1 tbsp. Coffee paste or Chocolate paste
- Extra Kao fen for dusting
- 375 g. Coffee lotus paste, divide into 15 portions, 25g each

Directions:

- Mix the Kao fen and snow skin in an average-sized container and keep.
- Mix the icing sugar and Crisco and boil. Allow the ingredients to melt and put off the heat, stir and add ½ tsp. Kahlua liquor.
- Pour a hot liquid mixture into the flour, stir the mix until the dough is soft.
- Portion the dough into 15 and shape it into a ball.
- Dust with some Kao fen and press into the mold. Unmold to store in a container.

PECAN MOONCAKE

Preparation Time: 45 mins.

Cooking Time: 10 mins.

Servings: 4

Ingredients:

- 160 g. butter
- 200 g. low-gluten flour
- 50 g. pecan powder
- 70 g. refined sugar
- 2 g. sea salt
- 50 ml. milk
- An appropriate amount of pecan nuts.

Directions:

- To make the pecan nuts aromatic, roast them at 150°C for 10 minutes. This will be a difficult chore, but you're ready to begin after the nuts are roasted. Remove from the oven and set aside to cool for later use
- While some individuals prefer not to toast their nuts, toasting them will give you an advantage over the competition. However, if possible, toast your nuts first and then cut them once they've been roasted. This will keep you from burning. You can make them work efficiently if you learn the technique of toasting them.
- Place the granulated sugar in the milk, microwave for one minute, and stir until the sugar melts. You want it to be warm but not scorching.
- Put 50g of toasted nuts in a food processor to break down.

VANILLA MOONCAKE

Preparation Time: 2 hrs.

Cooking Time: 30 mins.

Servings: 25

Ingredients:

- 6 tbsp. cornstarch
- 2 tbsp. all-purpose flour
- ½ c. granulated sugar
- 5 large egg yolk

- 2 c. whole milk
- 2 tbsp. Butter
- ½ tsp. vanilla extract
- ⅓ c. vegetable oil
- ½ tsp. vanilla extract

Directions:

- Get a medium-sized bowl and mix the corn starch, half of the sugar, and all-purpose flour
- Whisk your egg yolk in a separate bowl
- Add the milk and another half of the sugar into a small-sized saucepan. Heat over moderate heat and stir constantly. Heat until about 49°C
- Observe that the milk is warm and add the dry ingredients in the first step above. Divide the egg-yolk into four parts and Add the warm milk to the egg yolk mixture set aside
- Heat and stir constantly until the mixture thickens.
- Remove the pot from the heater and add butter and vanilla extracts and mix well. Smoothen the texture and chill the custard in the freezer for 30 minutes.
- Prepare the mooncake dough by mixing the glutinous rice flour, rice flour, and corn starch and mix well with a fork. Add milk, oil, and vanilla extract into a small bowl and stir.
- Prepare a steamer (1-inch water into the pot), place the rack over the boiling pot, and leave for 15 to 20 minutes. A spoon inserted in the middle of the dough that comes out clean will show that it's done.
- Transfer and Cool off.
- Knead it using a spoon and form a dough ball
- Wrap the dough with the plastic wrap and chill in the fridge for 30 minutes
- Mold the mooncake by making the patterned side facing downward. Dust the mooncake with a thin layer of cornstarch. Press the dough into the mooncake, and your mooncakes are ready to eat!

LOTUS FLOWER MOONCAKE

Preparation Time: 1 hr.

Cooking Time: 10 mins.

Servings: 10

Ingredients:

- 120 g. all-purpose flour
- 40 g. bread flour (or high protein flour)
- 1 tbsp. sugar

- 30 g. margarine
- 20 g. shortening
- ⅓ c. water
- 100 g. all-purpose flour
- 65 g. shortening
- 300 g. red bean paste (or lotus paste)

Directions:

- Prepare the mooncake fillings by rolling a mixture of red bean cake /into ten equal pieces.
- Mix the ingredients thoroughly, then prepare the mooncake skin by mixing all ingredients for the water dough and kneading it until it becomes soft enough. Keep the water dough for 20 minutes and divide the rest into ten equal pieces 30d each.
- Prepare the oil dough ingredients and mix well enough and also portion the oil dough into ten as well 15g each is okay
- Wrap the oil dough inside the water dough for each of the cakes, roll the wrapped dough flat
- Cover and allow the dough to rest for about 10 minutes, cut the rolled dough into halves and keep the fillings inside one, place the cut dough on top of each other, then wrap the red bean filling and adjust the dough to cover the seam.
- Roll the dough into a ball and design four lines on top of it with a little knife
- Heat the oil in the wok hot and gently place the mooncake into the hot oil, making sure that the mooncake is submerged fully. Reduce heat to deep-fry the cake to a golden-brown color.

CHAPTER 3: MODERN MOONCAKES RECIPES

NO-BAKE MOONCAKES

Preparation Time: None

Cooking Time: None

Servings: 24

Ingredients:

- 100 g. cooked glutinous rice flour
- 40 g. icing sugar
- 65 ml. water
- 15 g. vegetable shortening
- Food colouring of choice
- Lotus/red bean paste for filling from Jia Yuan Supermarket
- Mooncake mould stamp

Directions:

- Mix 100g of flour and 40g of icing sugar in a large bowl. Add 15g shortening to the mixture.
- Add 65 ml of cold water to the mixture and knead until it's smooth. Cut the dough into two and add colorant to the two portions of the dough
- Flatten it into a round disc. Roll into balls the lotus filling.
- Wrap the fillings in the wrapper and seal completely.

- Place the ball in the mooncake mold.

SEAFOOD MOONCAKES

Preparation Time: 20 mins.

Cooking Time: 30 mins.

Servings: 10

Ingredients:

- 237 ml. all-purpose flour
- One pinch salt
- One egg lightly beaten
- 20 ml. milk plus 1 tbsp.
- 226.8 g. monkfish
- Six scallops
- 177 ml. milk
- Two garlic cloves
- 226.8 g. shrimp shelled
- 30 ml. butter
- 45 ml. all-purpose flour
- 59 ml. light cream
- 237 ml. gruyere cheese
- 30 ml. parsley leaves
- 1 salt and black pepper
- 23 ml. vegetable oil

Directions:

- Make pancake better, mixing flour and salt. Make a wellness center and pour the egg, four tsp. of oil, and a cup of milk.
- Remove skin from the fish. Add ¾ milk into the saucepan, garlic. Add all fish except shrimp. Once the shrimp turns pink, remove all the seafood and keep. Strain the garlic/fish milk.
- Add butter to the saucepan and melt until bubbling subsides. Whisk in the flour and cook for 2 min. Whisk the reserved milk and the cream. Reduce the heat, add cheese, parsley, and season to taste with salt and white pepper. Add seafood and stir gently.
- Preset the oven to 180°C. Heat a skillet over high heat. Grease it with a small amount of oil.
- Whisk the pancake and add three tbsp. into the skillet. Cover the bottom of the pan with batter.

- Wrap the fillings in the Pancake and fold the side. Place in the oven until the pancake is heated through.

CRYSTAL SKIN MOONCAKES

Preparation Time: 1 hr.

Cooking Time: 20 mins.

Servings: 16

Ingredients:

- 2 packs crystal mooncake powder
- 2 packs custard filling
- 2 packs white sugar (for making syrup)
- 2 trays silicone crystal mooncake mould

Directions:

- Share the custard fillings into 16 portions.
- Mix the two packs of crystal mooncake powder with 200ml cold water to achieve a smooth paste.
- Combine two packs of sugar with 400ml water and boil until dissolved. Cool slightly.
- Add crystal mooncake into the heat-resistant container and position the container over a pan of hot water.
- Boil the water and keep stirring the mooncake paste until it thickens. Stop the heat.
- Brush silicon mold with corn oil.
- Fill the mooncake mold halfway with the thickened paste.
- Steam under high heat for 5-10 minutes. Cool and remove from the mold.

SNOW SKIN MOONCAKES

Preparation Time: 15 mins.

Cooking Time: 1 hr.

Servings: 8

Ingredients:

- 1 kg. glutinous rice
- ½ kg. icing sugar
- 200 ml. vegetable oil
- 400 ml. milk
- Food coloring
- Chestnut puree, as needed
- Red bean, as needed

- Food essence, as needed

Directions:

- Preheat flour on the baking sheet and bake for 30 minutes. Stir flour every 5-10minutes. To define the flour is cooked or not.
- Separate the flour to cool.
- Get ½ c. of cooked flour ready to dust the molded mooncake.
- Allow the cooked flour to be half-cooled, then mix with milk, oil, and icing sugar until a paste/dough is formed.
- Dust the mold with ½ c. of cooked flour.
- Make a roll of the paste above and the fillings (red bean and chestnut puree). Flatten the paste ball and the paste rolls and place the fillings rolls in the middle. Close the flattened paste ball.
- Seam to seal and paste into the mold, press with your palm. Knock slightly and turn mold on the plate.

CARROT MOONCAKES

Preparation Time: 25 mins.

Cooking Time: 20 mins.

Servings: 10

Ingredients:

- 40 g. glutinous rice flour
- 35 g. rice flour
- 15 g. wheat starch
- 35 g. icing sugar
- 145 g. carrot milk*
- 30 g. cooking oil
- 240 g. black sesame paste

Directions:

- Combine 50g of carrot and 150g of milk and blend the mixture to extract 145g of carrot milk
- Bring all the ingredients together in the same container and mix them thoroughly until they become smooth. Sieve the mixture into an oil-coated bowl, put it in a steamer, and apply heat for about 25 minutes until it steams.
- Stir with a spatula for 3 minutes when hot. Cool it for about 10 minutes under room temperature, then wrap with cling wrap and pass it to the refrigerator to chill for 30-35 minutes.

For the Hand-Coating Flour:

- Stir fry one tbsp. of glutinous rice in a dry pot under medium-low heat for about 5minutes and put aside to cool
- Share the paste into eight equal portions
- Adjust the snow skin into a flat round shape and fill it, wrapping the filling with snow skin. Use your hand to coat with flour to form a small mooncake mold
- Keep it in the refrigerator to cool for about an hour before Servings to bring out a better texture. Make sure to use an airtight container for your storage.

GREEN TEA MOONCAKES

Preparation Time: 15 mins.

Cooking Time: 40 mins.

Servings: 10

Ingredients:

- 150 g. split mung bean (soak for 3 hours, drained)
- 2 tbsp. Matcha powder (Japanese green tea powder)
- 4 tbsp. Hot water
- ¼ tsp. fine salt
- 120 g. fine sugar
- 200 g. milk
- 2 tbsp. glutinous rice flour
- 40 g. cooking oil

Directions:

- Apply moderate heat to Steam the already soaked bean until it becomes very soft for 30 minutes.

- Prepare a paste from the mixture of matcha powder with hot water. Add in salt, sugar, and milk well. Combine the glutinous rice flour and mix thoroughly. Add in the steamed split mung bean and blend all to achieve a smooth texture, then sieve into a separate pan
- Put cooking oil into the mixture and mix well
- Cooke for 10 minutes under moderate heat, lower the heat, and cook for another 10 minutes until you have a smooth paste.
- Keep it on one side for complete cooling. Store the paste in a separate container and freeze it, and always keep it at room temperature before use.

MULTI-GRAIN MOONCAKES

Preparation Time: 1 hr.

Cooking Time: 10 mins.

Servings: 10

Ingredients:

- ½ Assorted Nuts, roughly chopped
- ⅔ c. Ground Old Fashioned Rolled Oats
- ½ c. Multigrain Flour
- 3 tbsp. Hot water
- ½ tbsp. Vegetable oil
- 1 c. Unsweetened Cocoa powder
- 1 tbsp. water, room temperature

Directions:

- Keep the Old-Fashioned Rolled Oats, Multigrain Flour, Vegetable Oil, and water 3 tbsp. in a bowl, mix them, knead them well to form a dough, and divide them into 10-12 balls.
- Take the Unsweetened cocoa powder, assorted nuts, and water and knead them well. Divide them into 12 parts.
- Occupy the dough with the fillings and shape using the mooncake mold. Rub the mold with some oil before placing it.
- Store the mooncake in the refrigerator for a minimum of one hour before consumption.

FERRERO ROCHER BROWNIE

Preparation Time: 15 mins.

Cooking Time: 45 mins.

Servings: 16

Ingredients:

- 100 g. dark, roughly chopped chocolate
- 113 g. saltless butter, room temperature
- Three large eggs
- 1 c. white granulated sugar
- 50 g. packed dark brown sugar
- 1 ½ tsp. Vanilla extract
- ¾ c. of plain flour
- ¼ c. unsweetened cocoa
- ¼ tsp. salt
- 16 Unwrapped Ferrero Rocher
- ¼ c. Nutella spread

Directions:

- Keep the oven at 160°C and grease. Line a square baking tin with baking paper.
- Position the butter and chocolate in the heat resistant bowl and microwave for about 30 seconds at an instant, stirring between each until it is well mixed and smooth.
- Whisk sugar and egg separately in a large bowl
- Add the already melted chocolate, vanilla, and butter and beat together
- Add flour, salt and cocoa, then beat until all are thoroughly combined
- Pour them into the tin and press the Ferrero Rocher into the batter, spaced evenly.
- Heat the Nutella for 30 seconds, then pour it over the top of the brownie batter.
- Take between 40-45 minutes to bake.
- Cool slowly at room temperature before cutting into them. You can also use the fridge to accelerate the process.

SALTED EGG YOLK CUSTARD MOONCAKES

Preparation Time: 20 mins.

Cooking Time: 30 mins.

Servings: 20

Ingredients:

- 35 g. cake flour
- 76 g. custard powder

- 35 g. milk powder
- 200 g. sugar
- 70 ml. evaporated milk or full-fat milk
- 170 ml. coconut milk
- 2 eggs (kept for egg wash)
- 300 g. unsalted butter
- 5-6 salted egg yolk (optional)
- 500 g. cake flour
- 220 g. unsalted butter
- 1 egg
- One tiny bit of dark soy sauce for egg wash
- 1 tsp. honey for glaze

Directions:

- Make the salted egg yolk custard filling.
- Steam 5-6 salted eggs are already rolled in little oil for 15 minutes, crushing them with a fork and keeping one side.
- Combine all the dry ingredients. Add evaporated milk, coconut milk, the two eggs kept, and the softened butter to the dry ingredients and mix thoroughly but keep the egg yolk on one side.
- Steam the custard for about 20 minutes.
- You will observe a layer of oil after the steaming, and while the filling is hot, mix the butter /oil with the crushed egg yolk, bake to the filling, and when cooled, place it on a plastic wrap from a long log shape. Make sure it is well wrapped to prevent leakage. Cool for 2 hours and utilize this period to make the mooncake crust pastry.
- Follow the steps above for the moon cake pastry, too, since they are the same sets of ingredients. After the final stage of chilling this for at least two hours in the fridge, share the crust and filling into two equal portions and measure their weight.
- Get a large baking surface and position your parchment paper on it so you can easily place your mooncakes on it after stamping with the mould.
- Put a piece of crust pastry onto a little piece of plastic wrap and roll flat to achieve a circle of about 3-3.5 inch
- Put a piece of custard filling on the smoothened crust pastry. Arrange the sides of the plastic wrap and adjust it to form a tight ball. Dust the dough with some flour and place it into the mould.
- Allow the mooncake to admit the shape of the mould and chill the mooncake for 30 minutes.
- Brush the chilled mooncake with the egg wash and save the rest for second brushing. Keep the oven at 450°F for 6 mins. Place the mooncakes in the middle rack of the oven during baking. Take the mooncake out and cool down.
- Perform the second brushing with the egg wash and bake for 6 mins at 450 F. Mix 1 tsp. of honey with some hot water in a small bowl, brush the warm mooncakes with the honey glaze, and let the mooncake cool down a bit.

BLACK SESAME MOONCAKES

Preparation Time: 35 mins.

Cooking Time: 20 mins.

Servings: 16

Ingredients:

- 20 g. Freshly ground black sesame powder
- 190 g. Cake flour
- 100 g. Unsalted butter
- 15 g. Egg wash
- 45 g. Icing sugar
- 20 g. whipping cream
- 10 g. Coconut milk

For the Filling:

- 216 g. Black sesame mooncake filling
- 24 g. Freshly ground black sesame powder

Directions:

- Roast sesame seeds over a slight heat in a big bottom pan with constant stirring until the fragrant starts popping. Allow it to cool completely.
- Grind it either manually with mortar and pestle or using a food processor until the oils is extracted when it forms a paste.
- Add ¼ c. of glutinous rice flour and process it until the paste comes together, hold together, and refrigerate. Mix the sesame powder with cake flour.
- Subject butter to room temperature and mix the icing sugar and sieve. Mix the egg wash, whipping cream, and coconut milk together, knead well, wrap in cling film, and cool in the refrigerator.
- Remove the pastry dough from the refrigerator and knead to 28g each.
- Flatten it with a rolling pin under cling film. Wrap one of the sesames filling in the dough.
- Mold the mooncake, dust it with flour, knead, and place it in the mold. Refrigerate and press for an hour.
- Remove and spray water on the mooncake and place them on the baking tray. Baking should occur at 200°C for 4 minutes and 180°C for 2 minutes. Remove the baking tray and brush on syrup, and bake for another one min.

ALMONDS MOONCAKES

Preparation Time: 20 mins.

Cooking Time: 35 mins.

Servings: 11-15

Ingredients:

- Two packet sweet almond-flavored biscuits
- 100 g. almond saffron powder
- One sachet Eno
- 300 ml. milk
- Greasing oil
- One packet gem
- 100 g. Coconut powder
- 50 g. duty fruity
- 2 tbsp. milkmaid

Directions:

- Combine ground biscuit, almond, milkmaid and prepare a batter using milk. Add tutti fruity and Eno.
- Keep the batter in a greased cake tin and cook for 35 minutes. Maintain 180°C temperature in the microwave.
- Cut the center part of the cake and garnish it with coconut powder to achieve the look of a smiling moon.
- Shape the upper part to the sky, add jam and garnish it with gems.
- Serve and enjoy.

COLORFUL SNOW SKIN MOONCAKES

Preparation Time: 30 mins.

Cooking Time: 12 mins.

Servings: 8

Ingredients:

- 65 g. Koh fun cooked glutinous flour
- 40 g. icing sugar
- 50 ml. coconut milk warmed
- 7 g. coconut oil at room temperature
- 1 tsp. Suncore Butterfly Pea Superjuice Powder
- ½ tsp. red yeast rice
- 1 tsp. Suncore Pink Pitaya Superjuice Powder
- 1 tsp. Suncore Emerald Pandan Superjuice Powder
- 240 g. lotus seed paste filling

Directions:

- Make the Koh fun by setting the oven temperature to 93°C. Put the flour together and position it on the baking sheet lined with parchment paper. Then remove from the oven.
- Share the lotus paste filling into eight equal balls of about the same size
- Mix the Koh fun, icing sugar warmed coconut milk and coconut oil together and knead to form a smooth dough, and divide the dough into four portions of different colors of your choices.

RAINBOW SODA SNOW SKIN MOONCAKES

Preparation Time: 20 mins.

Cooking Time: 30 mins.

Servings: 12

Ingredients:

- 90 g. fried glutinous rice flour
- 10 g. wheat starch
- 30 g. shortening
- 40 g. powdered sugar
- 200 g. ice-cream soda or 7-up
- A little pandan (green), pink, and lemon-yellow food colouring
- 600 g. Lotus paste
- 30 g. Melon seeds for fillings

Directions:

- Make a mold from starch and rice flour. Add icing sugar and shortening and mix till it is well mixed.
- Pour in ice-cream soda and mix to achieve a soft dough. Share the dough into four equal portions and add colorants to three portions. Leave the remaining one white.
- Form an equal-sized rectangular shape from the dough, stack them on one another, and then roll into a Swiss roll.
- Cut into six equal pieces and divide the lotus paste fillings into six portions. Roll the spiral part flat and wrap it with the lotus paste filling. Fill into the mold, then knockout.
- Cool it in the refrigerator before serving.

MINI SNOW SKIN MOONCAKES

Preparation Time: 60 mins.

Cooking Time: 30 mins.

Servings: 5

Ingredients:

For the Snow Skin:

- 45 g. glutinous rice flour
- 30 g. rice flour

- 30 g. wheat starch
- 42 g. icing sugars
- 145 g. milk
- 25 g. condensed milk
- 25 g. vegetable oil
- Water

For the Taro Filling:

- 140 g. taro (cooked)
- 70 g. water
- 45 g. sugar
- Pinch of salt
- 23 g. vegetable oil
- 50 g. fresh cream
- 20 g. glutinous rice flour
- 25 g. glutinous rice flour (cooked)
- 25 g. glutinous rice flour (cooked)

Directions:

- Combine all the Snow Skin ingredients in a big bowl. Mix thoroughly. Add milk, condensed milk veg oil, mix well. Steam the mixture over moderate heat for 20 minutes or until it is cooked. Transfer the dough to a mixer running at a medium speed for about 5 minutes until it's perceived smooth. Wrap the dough with a tight wrap and keep it in the fridge for about 1.5 hours.
- Bring all the Taro ingredients together and mix well to smoothen it. Transfer the mixture into a pan and cook the mixture over moderate heat and constant stirring until a dough is formed. Refrigerate for one hour
- Divide the filling and the snow skin in equal ratios and roll them into balls. Use the rice flour to coat the snow skin and coat the mooncake with the glutinous rice flour using mooncake mold to carve the shape.

BANANA MOONCAKES

Preparation Time: 5 mins.

Cooking Time: 40 mins.

Servings: 12

Ingredients:

- 4 ripe bananas

- 10 Medjool dates
- 2 eggs
- ½ tsp. Ginger
- ¼ tsp. Ground cloves
- ½ tsp. cinnamon
- 1 tsp. Vanilla Bean Paste
- 250 g. gluten-free flour, quirky cooking cookbook
- 50 g. walnuts
- 1 tsp. Bi-carb soda
- One pinch salt
- 40 g. honey

Directions:

- Set the oven to 180°C and grease a loaf pan. Add bananas, dates, eggs, ginger, ground cloves, cinnamon, and vanilla to a big bowl.
- Mix at a moderate speed for 20 seconds; combine flour, walnut, bi-card soda salt, and honey to the big bowl for further mixing at a moderate speed for another 2 minutes and pour into the mold.
- Bake at 180°C to achieve a clean skewer.

THOUSAND LAYER MOONCAKES

Preparation Time: 20 mins.

Cooking Time: 35 mins.

Servings: 6

Ingredients:

- 1 c. dried lotus seeds
- ¼ c. sugar
- ¼ c. oil
- ¾ c. + 1 tbsp. All-purpose flour
- ¼ c. + 2 tbsp. Vegetable shortening
- ¾ c. + 2 tbsp. all-purpose flour
- 1 ½ tsp. food-grade matcha powder
- 1 tbsp. sugar
- 3 tbsp. vegetable shortening
- ½ c. water

Directions:

- Line a medium plate with parchment paper. Using a one ½ tbsp. Cookie scoop, portion out six scoops of white lotus paste and drop onto the parchment. Freeze the paste until solid, at least 45 minutes or overnight (cover if freezing overnight).
- Combine all the ingredients to make the water dough and refrigerate for 30 minutes.
- Combine all the ingredients into the oil dough and refrigerate for 30 minutes.
- Prepare the oven keeping it at 400°F, and line in a large, rimmed baking sheet with parchment paper.
- Divide the oil and water dough into three equal parts, each making (6 portions) and taking the weight. Dust with flour, roll individual portions of the oil dough into a smooth ball, expand the eater dough into a 4-inch round, and work with one pair at a Time.
- Position an oil dough ball on the water-dough round and connect the edges to cover each other completely. Adjust the dough until you get the edges of the dough pinched together to seal fully. Position the mooncake on the prepared baking sheet and repeat the process for the remaining dough.
- Bake until it turns flaky and slightly golden, about 25 to 28 minutes, then cool the mooncakes there.
- Serve it warm or at room temperature.

PORK FILLED CHINESE MOONCAKES

Preparation Time: 20 mins.

Cooking Time: 30 mins.

Servings: 10

Ingredients:

- 2 oz. Ginger, freshly chopped
- 1 ½ all-purpose flour
- 2 tbsp. unflavored lard
- ½ table salt
- ¼ c. ginger water
- 1 c. cake flour
- 3 tbsp. lard, unflavored variety
- 1 lb. ground pork
- ½ tsp. salt, table variety
- 1 tbsp. tamari
- 1 tbsp. sesame

- ½ freshly ground black pepper
- 4 tbsp. scallions, finely chopped
- 1 tbsp. dry sherry
- Egg wash

Directions:

- Mix all ingredients in a pot and bubble gently for 15 minutes to make the ginger water. Let it strain through the mesh strainer and dispose of the solid. Cool it in the refrigerator.
- Prepare the lard dough by adding all the ingredients together, then add the ginger water little by little and knead the dough to smoothness.
- Mix the flour thoroughly with the lard to obtain the cake lard.
- Mix all the filling ingredients in a bowl and mix well.
- Share the dough into ten equal parts each.
- Form ten different dough pieces.
- Carefully wrap your lard dough around the balls of cake dough to form a bigger ball.
- Add one-tenth of the fillings to the dough. In the middle of the dough around the filings, gather all the edges and close.
- Keep the rack in the middle position and heat the oven to 190°C. Whisk the egg and brush over the top part of the mooncakes and bake until it turns golden brown for 20 minutes and serves hot.

APPLE PECAN SPRING ROLL MOONCAKES

Preparation Time: 5 mins.

Cooking Time: 45 mins.

Servings: 4

Ingredients:

- 3 small apples, chopped
- ½ tsp. fresh lime zest, finely grated
- 2 ½ tsp. fresh lime juice
- One beaten Egg
- 1 tsp. cinnamon
- 1 ½ tsp. vanilla extract
- Star anise
- 1 tsp. raw granulated sugar
- One cooking spray

- 1 c. Pecans
- ½ c. melted vegan butter
- 8 spring rolls

Directions:

- Preheat the oven and keep the temperature at 375 F.
- Heat pecans in a dry pan for 3 minutes to reach golden color. Remove from the pan and chop to a reasonable size.
- Combine butter, star anise, apples, cinnamon, sugar, and cook for about 5 minutes on low heat until the apple becomes soft. Add the pecans and stir.
- Oil your cupcake molds the place about ¼ of the apple and pecan fillings into the double spring roll wrapper lined cupcake and handle gently.
- Use the beaten egg to seal the mooncake at the bottom. Brush the mooncakes with allowing the sealed session to face up.
- Bake for 15 minutes. Remove from the oven when done. Brush the mooncake top with egg again and bake for another 15 minutes until you notice a golden-brown color.
- Serve hot.

PLAIN LOTUS PASTE WITH SALTED EGG YOLK

Preparation Time: 12 hrs.

Cooking Time: 2 hrs.

Servings: 18

Ingredients:

- 1 c. + 2 tsp. granulated sugar
- ½ c. of water
- Juice of ½ a lemon

- 12 oz. dried lotus seeds
- 4 c. of water
- 1 ⅔ c. powdered sugar
- 1 ¼ c. peanut oil
- ⅓ c. maltose
- 12 salted duck egg yolks
- 8 ¾ tbsp. sugar syrup
- ⅓ peanut oil
- 1 tsp. lye water
- 1 ¾ c. of flour
- 1 egg yolk
- 3 tbsp. water

Directions:

- Prepare amber color sugary liquid by heating the sugar and water in a saucepan over moderate heat and constant stirring. When it boils, stir in Lemon juice and lower the temperature immediately. Stop stirring and uncover the syrup simmer for 60-70minutes. Allow it to cool and form caramel before storing it in the refrigerator.
- Prepare the lotus paste.
- Prepare the salted duck egg yolk.
- Make the dough by combining a sugar syrup, oil, and lye water mixed with flour using a rubber spatula to fold it into a soft dough, cover it in an airtight container, and cool for one hour.
- Prepare the filling and shape each portion of the filling into balls. Take one lotus ball, make a deep hole inside, insert one duck egg yolk, and then close and reshape.
- Prepare the mooncake mold. Take on a dough ball, dust it with flour, perfect it on the lightly floured surface, and close the dough around the filling without capturing air inside.
- Set the oven to 160°C Preheated temperature, spray the oven with a food-grade spray. Put the mooncake in the oven and bake for 5 minutes. Take them out of the oven, reduce the temperature to 150°C and bake for another 15 minutes.

CHARCOAL BAMBOO MOONCAKES

Preparation Time: 1 hr.

Cooking Time: 25 mins.

Servings: 10

Ingredients:

For the Mooncake:

- 175 g. golden syrup
- 1 tsp. lye water
- 55 g. peanut oil
- ⅛ tsp. baking soda
- 7 g. charcoal powder
- 240 g. all-purpose flour
- Egg wash: 1 egg yolk, 1 ½ tbsp. water

For the Filling:

- 1200 g. lotus seed paste
- 10 salted egg yolks, baked
- 40 g. toasted melon seeds

Directions:

For the Mooncake Dough Skin:

- Prepare all ingredients.
- In a mixing bowl, pour golden syrup then peanut oil to make mooncake skin. Then add lye water, baking soda, all-purpose flour, and bamboo charcoal powder.
- Using a spatula, stir until a soft, smooth dough forms.
- With saran wrap, cover the mixing bowl and set aside for 30 minutes.
- After 30 minutes, divide into 10 equal pieces.

For the Lotus Seed Paste Fillings:

- Mix lotus seed paste with toasted melon seeds until they are well combined.
- Roll into a long log and cut into 10 pieces using a sharp knife. Then roll into a ball weighing about 120g.
- Flatten the lotus seed paste ball before placing the egg yolk in the middle. Wrap and roll to form a ball. You should obtain at least 10 dough balls, each weighing about 135g. Set aside.

For the Mooncakes:

- Slightly flatten the dough skin, then wrap it around the filling. Slowly push the dough skin until it covers the entire filling. Then roll to a ball.
- Dust the wrapped dough lightly and place it into a mooncake mold. Repeat the process for the other wrapped doughs.
- Place the mooncakes on a baking tray and bake in a preheated 200°c oven for 10 minutes.
- Remove and cool on a wire rack for 10-15 minutes. Lightly brush the tops of the mooncakes with egg wash.
- Return the mooncakes to the oven and continue baking at the same temperature for 10 more minutes.

- Let mooncakes cool when done. You can store it in an air-tight container for 2 days before serving to soften and let the flavor develop.
- Serve with freshly brewed tea and enjoy!

ORANGE MOONCAKES

Preparation Time: 2 hrs.

Cooking Time: 10 mins.

Servings: 16

Ingredients:

- 120 g. Kao fen
- 50 g. Hong Kong flour
- 65 g. icing sugar
- 30 g. shortening premium
- 1 orange
- 155 g. orange juice
- 2 tbsp. Sugar syrup (if orange is not sweet)
- 500 g. Sweet corn Paste
- 60 g. Sunflower seeds
- ½ tsp. orange essence
- Water, for blending juices

Directions:

- Preset oven temperature to 180°C and bake Hong Kong Flour for 5 minutes. Stir regularly and bake for additional 5 minutes.
- Mix both the flour and icing sugar (sieved).
- Rinse Orange, grate the skin, peel, and remove the skin and seeds.
- Grind the orange slices, mix the orange zest, and combine with the orange juice. Weigh up to 155 g. Add the orange juice gently and mix well to achieve a smooth dough and confirm enough juice. Let it rest for about 20 minutes.
- Drop the sunflower seeds into the paste, make about 16 sweetcorn portions weighing 30g each, and keep one side. Apply some Hong Kong flour to the gloves to prevent sticking dough and make 16 balls.
- Adjust the dough, keeping a paste filling in the middle, and wrap. Pour HK flour into the tray and dust the mold too. Remove the mooncake from its mold, and you are done.
- Refrigerate well and serve chilled.

CHAPTER 4: TRADITIONAL MOONCAKES RECIPES

THERMOMIX TRADITIONAL MOONCAKES

Preparation Time: 1 hr.

Cooking Time: 25 mins.

Servings: 7

Ingredients:

- 150 g. Prima Hong Kong Flour
- 90 g. Golden syrup
- 32 g. Peanut oil
- ¼ tsp. Alkaline water
- Filling of choice
- 1 egg yolk + 1 tsp. milk

Directions:

- Add sieved flour into a mixing bowl

HALAL MOONCAKES

Preparation Time: 20 mins.

Cooking Time: 30 mins.

Servings: 18

Ingredients:

For the Water Oil Crust:

- 204 g. whole wheat flour
- 21 g. fine sugar
- 96 g. water
- 54 g. vegetable oil

For the Oil Crust:

- 180 g. whole wheat flour
- 90 g. vegetable oil

For the Fillings:

- 500 g. minced beef
- 5 g. pepper powder
- 15 ml. soy sauce
- 5 g. salt
- 10 ml. sesame oil
- 1 quail egg
- 10 g. chopped scallions

Directions:

- Prepare filings by mixing the fillings ingredients. Divide into round balls and store them in the refrigerator for an hour.
- Prepare water Oil crust by mixing all the ingredients, kneading thoroughly, and then sharing them into smaller doughs. Let them relax for at least 10 minutes.
- Prepare oil crust following the previous step above.

Mix the Crust:

- Stretch out the water-oil crust, wrap it in the oil crust dough, and adjust it with a rolling pin.
- Cover them with a damp cloth, relax them for 15 minutes, roll again upside down, and relax for 20 minutes.

Prepare the Wrappers:

- Bake them in the oven between 170-180°C temperature for 15 minutes. Turn over and bake for another 8 minutes, then another 8 minutes again.
- The filings are ready to be served.

YUNNAN MOONCAKES

Preparation Time: 30 mins.

Cooking Time: 30 mins.

Servings: 8

Ingredients:

For the Dough:

- 30 g. Honey
- 25 g. Sugar
- ¼ tsp. Baking Soda
- ½ tsp. Baking Powder
- 60 g. Water
- 30 g. Oil
- 200 g. All-Purpose Flour

For the Stuffed Pork Leg:

- 150 g. Waxed Pork Leg
- 30 g. All-Purpose Flour
- 30 g. Honey
- 20 g. Sugar
- 20 g. Oil

Directions:

For the Dough:

- Mix all the ingredients well without the oil and flour.
- Combine a portion of the flour separately with the oil and the remaining on the clean working surface and mix properly with the honey mixture.
- Add the oil and flour paste and knead for 5-7 mins then cover and allow it to rest for 30 minutes

For the Stuffed Pork Leg:

- Boil the waxed pork leg for 15 minutes till it turns light brown. Toast the flour for about 3-4 min to achieve a light brown color. Chop the pork leg and keep it in a bowl. Now, add the toasted flour, sugar, honey, and oil. Mix thoroughly. Share into eight equal portions.
- Also, dress the dough into eight equal portions of small balls and hide it in a plastic wrap. Make a hole in the first dough, fill it with the pork leg, and close the shape.
- Bake at a specified temperature of 200°C (20min).

SAKURA SNOW SKIN MOONCAKES

Preparation Time: 45 mins

Cooking Time: 5 mins

Servings: 4

- 25 g. Kao fen (cooked glutinous rice flour)
- 115 g. Snow skin flour
- 25 g. Icing sugar sifted
- 23 g. Crisco
- 150 g. Water (boil 220g water with two pandan leaves, leave to cool) and measure 150 g. water.
- Some extra Kao fen for dusting
- 150 g. Cherry Blossom Paste
- 5 Pickled Sakura Cherry Blossoms

Directions:

- Blend the Kao fen and snow skin flour in a bowl and keep.
- Bring two pandan leaves water, icing sugar, and shortening together; heat them in a pot, allow them to boil, and stir until shortening melts.
- Pour the hot liquid on the floor and use a spatula stir the mixture to succulent dough and allow it to cool.
- Weigh 26g dough and wrap it up in 30g cherry blossom
- Form a ball from it and position the Sakura on top. Immerse the ball into the Kao fen and roll the ball gentry to circulate the Kao fen dust.
- Force into the mold. Unmold and keep the mooncake in an air-tight container
- Cool snow skin mooncakes before consumption.

SHANGHAINESE MOONCAKES

Preparation Time: 1 hr.

Cooking Time: 25 mins

Servings: 10

Ingredients:

- 125 g. all-purpose flour
- 10 g. icing sugar
- 20 g. milk powder
- ⅛ tsp. salt
- 64g. unsalted softened butter
- 1 large egg
- 1 bean paste
- 25 g. melon seed

Directions:

- Get a dry pan and pour the melon seed. Allow it to toast until slightly brown and keep it on one side to cool.
- Make the bean paste or other choice sweet paste preferably a day before. Weigh and share into equal portions for filling.
- Mix the bean paste with the toasted melon seeds.
- Make the dough by combining all the dry ingredients in the mixing bowl, adding the softened butter, rub the butter until you have a crumbly texture. Add egg and proceed with the kneading to achieve a soft, smooth ball
- After chilling in the fridge, preheat the oven to 350F, portion each dough to about equal sizes making sure that they are covered while you work on one dough at a Time. Establish the filling in the middle of each dough and refrigerate
- Offload it from the fridge, brush the egg wash, and sprinkle it with some sesame or melon seeds. Gently retain them. Do not brush with egg wash to prevent imprints on the final products if you use a mooncake mold.
- Retain in the oven for 15 minutes and brush with egg wash to complete the time. Bake again for another 10-15 minutes to achieve a golden-brown color. Cool for 5 min on the Baking sheet and pass to the cooling rack for complete cooling

HOPIA MOONCAKES

Preparation Time: 30 mins.

Cooking Time: 30 mins.

Servings: 6

Ingredients:

- 3 c. Flour
- ½ c. shortening
- ½ c. water
- ½ c. oil c.
- 2 tbsp. corn syrup
- 1 Pack of moon beans
- 3-4 c. of water
- 2-2 ½ c. of sugar

Directions:

- Combine the shortening and one c. of flour, mix until it completely blends, and refrigerate for 30 minutes. Add the ingredients left to the chilled mixture.
- The dough should be slightly oily to the touch and solid. Share the dough into 50 g. ball, straighten the ball, add a small ball of filling in the middle part and adjust it to form a disk.
- Boil a mixture of moon beans and water in a deep skillet, reduce the heat, and simmer. Stir continuously. When the beans turn soft, add sugar and continue stirring and when the water dries off, transfer to a container and cool. Bake for 20-25 mins at 325°C. Brush after 10 minutes with egg wash and proceed with baking.

SUZHOU STYLE MOONCAKES

Preparation Time: 15 mins.

Cooking Time: 20 mins.

Servings: 8

Ingredients:

- 100 g. plain flour
- 50 g. vegetable
- 30 g. vegetable shortening or lard or peanut
- 50 g. plain water
- 3 g. salt
- 300 g. minced pork
- 3 stalks of spring onion
- 3 cm long fresh ginger
- 2 tbsp. of oyster sauce
- 1 tbsp. of light soya sauce
- 1 tbsp. of Chinese cooking wine

- 1 tbsp. of sesame oil
- ½ tbsp. of white pepper
- Dashes of salt

Directions:

- Preset the oven to 180°C and set the baking tray
- Gather all the filling ingredients together in a mixing bowl, squeeze the ginger juices and stir until completely mixed. Share into eight different portions.
- Mix all the water dough ingredients. In a separate bowl, stir and knead until well mixed. Also, share into eight different portions and set aside for 15 minutes.
- Prepare the oil dough too and knead. Rest for 15 minutes too
- Wrap the oil dough inside the water dough, seal, and form into a rectangular shape.
- Form a Swiss roll and flatten with a rolling pin and shake a meatball on the top center. Adjust it to a round shape such as a disc shape.
- Bake in a 108°C oven temperature for 10 minutes, turn cakes upside down for another 10 minutes and bake again to achieve a golden-brown color.

TEOCHEW MOONCAKES

Preparation Time: 50 mins

Cooking Time: 1 hr. 20 mins

Servings: 12

Ingredients:

For the Yam Paste:

- 600 g. yam peeled and sliced
- 180 g. granulated sugar
- 100 g. shallot oil
- 80 g. wheat starch flour
- 12 salted egg yolk

For the Oil Dough:

- 180 g. plain flour
- 80 g. shortening/butter/lard
- 30 ml. vegetable oil

- Pinch of salt

For the Water Dough:

- 220 g. plain flour
- 80 g. shortening /butter/lard
- 40 g. castor sugar
- 80 ml. water
- 1 tsp. purple sweet potato powder

Directions:

- Preparing the Yam paste involves steaming the peeled yam for 20 minutes to soften. Turn off the heat. Mash the hot yam with other ingredients with hot yam to form a paste with a stick blender.
- Heat the remaining 50 g shallot oil on moderate heat and add the yam paste. Allow it to remain for 10-15 minutes. Remove and keep cooling.
- Steam the salted egg yolk for filling on high heat for 10 minutes.
- Prepare the oven and set it to 180°C temperature.
- Share the yam paste into balls of equal sizes, prepare one of the balls and wrap around the salted eggs in 12 places.
- Make the dough in a bowl, add the flour, and mix until a soft dough is obtained. Allow it to rest for 20 mins.
- Prepare the water dough in another large bowl. Mix all the ingredients well enough until a soft dough is obtained and knead for 5 mins. Share into four equal parts and keep aside for 20 minutes.
- Combine the two doughs with the water dough wrapped around the oil dough
- Flatten the combined dough and cut into three, making 12 portions in all. Take one of the portions, flatten and put one yam paste ball in the center; seal the edges.
- Place it on a baking tray. Bake them in the oven at 180°C temperature for 20-25mins or until golden brown. Allow it to cool and serve.

TAIWANESE MOONCAKES

Preparation Time: 1 hr.

Cooking Time: 30 mins.

Servings: 12

Ingredients:

- 100 g. glutinous rice

- 30 g. cornstarch
- 30 g. granulated sugar
- 180 g. milk
- 15 g. milk
- 60 g. meat floss
- 12 salted egg yolk
- 360 g. taro past
- 110 g. all-purpose flour
- 20 g. icing sugar
- 40 g. shortening
- 50 ml. water
- 100 g. cake flour
- 40 g. butter
- One egg yolk
- 1 tsp. water
- Pinch of salt
- ¼ c. white Sesame seeds
- ¼ c. Black Sesame seeds

Directions:

- For raw, salted, steam egg yolks for 10 minutes over moderate heat and let them cool down.
- Divide already chilled Taro paste into 12 portions, roll into balls, and cover-up
- Prepare the mochi mixing all the ingredients, pour on a pan, and stir over a moderate heat
- Wrap plastic and chill it in the fridge for over 30 minutes
- Use a large mixing bowl, prepare the water dough by mixing flour with icing sugar, adding water, and continuing kneading until the color is evenly distributed. Keep aside for 30 minutes.
- Prepare the oil dough by rubbing the butter into the flour until it forms a smooth, soft dough with food coloring added
- Prepare the filling by flattening the taro paste into a circle and adding a portion of pork floss, salted egg yolk, and covering the entire taro paste
- Set the oven to 200 C. Divide the water and oil dough into six portions. Wrap the oil dough inside the water dough, cover, and keep for 30 minutes. Combine white and black sesame seeds in one bowl. Brush with egg, dip the bowl into the bowl containing sesame seeds, and prepare to bake.
- Keep the baking sheet inside the oven for about 30 minutes until the top becomes slightly golden-brown. Remove from the oven and cool.

CANTONESE-STYLE MOONCAKES

Preparation Time: 1 hr.

Cooking Time: 2 hrs.

Servings: 20

Ingredients:

- 120 g. dried Lotus seed
- 90 g. sugar
- 70 g. sunflower oil/peanut oil
- 159 g. invert syrup
- 50 g. sunflower oil
- ½ tsp. lye water
- 220 g. all-purpose flour
- Cornstarch for dusting
- One egg yolk
- One tsp. water
- 20 salted egg yolk

Directions:

- Soak dried lotus seed overnight, normally 30-40 minutes.
- Boil in excess water until soft (normally 30 – 40 minutes). Drain and generate a paste from it.
- Transfer the paste into a non-stick pan. Cook over moderate heat, add sugar and oil in batches while stirring until the paste dries, holds a shape, and cools.
- Prepare the dough by combining one egg yolk and some lotus seed paste. Weigh the filling and keep it at 30g. Adjust the paste into a round-shaped wrapper and keep the egg yolk at the center, further adjusting to seal it completely.
- Flatten 20g of dough into a wrapper. Use the previous step to make a ball around the filling.
- Shape and beautify the cakes, coating the ball with a thin layer of corn starch, keeping it in a mooncake mold, and placing it on a baking tray. Gently adjust it to shape.
- Maintain the oven at 160°C. Take the mooncakes, brush the top with a thin layer of egg wash, return them to the oven, bake for some 5 minutes more, remove, and brush with more egg wash, and proceed with the baking for another 10-15 minutes to achieve a brown color.

MATCHA COCONUT CUSTARD MOONCAKES

Preparation Time: 20 mins.

Cooking Time: 60 mins.

Servings: 5

Ingredients:

- 40 g. Glutinous rice flour
- 20 g. Rice flour
- 20 g. wheatstarch
- 10 g. plain flour
- 35 g. caster sugar
- 160 g. coconut milk
- 35 g. condensed milk
- ½ tsp. Matcha powder
- 30 ml. vegetable oil
- 20 g. custard powder
- 20 g. milk powder
- 60 g. Caster Sugar
- 30 g. Egg yolk
- 30 g. condensed milk
- 80 g. coconut cream
- 45 g. melted unsalted butter

Directions:

- To prepare the Snow skin, sieve the glutinous rice flour, corn/wheat starch, and flour in a medium heat resistance bowl, add sugar and mix, pour the coconut milk and condensed milk, then whisk to combine.
- Add vegetable oil and whisk until smooth. Cover and place in a steamer.

ADZUKI MOONCAKES

Preparation Time: 30 mins.

Cooking Time: 1 hr. 50 mins.

Servings: 8

Ingredients:

- ⅓ c. golden syrup
- 3 tbsp. peanut oil

- 1 c. cake flour
- ½ tsp. baking soda
- One pinch salt
- 1 ½ c. dry adzuki beans
- 4 c. of water
- ¼ c. peanut oil
- ¼ c. white sugar or more to taste
- 2 tbsp. wheat starch
- ½ c. all-purpose flour
- One egg yolk, beaten

Directions:

- Mix the golden syrup 3 tbsp. of peanut in a small pan and warm under low heat. Mix the cake flour, salt, and baking soda in a separate bowl. Keep stirring the golden syrup until it forms a smooth dough, then wrap well and refrigerate for 4 hours.
- Get a large saucepan containing water under a high amount of heat, pour the adzuki beans and boil. Keep at moderate heat, cover, and simmer until the beans become soft for about one hour. Drain and cool for ten minutes. Make a paste from the beans in the food processor.
- Using the previous saucepan, they heat ¼ c. of peanut oil at moderate temperature. Cook and stir until the beans paste attaches to the stirring spoon. Stir in the wheat starch and scrape into the mixing bowl. Chill in the fridge.
- Keep the oven temperature at 190°C and grease the baking sheet. Share the dough and the fillings each to 8 equal parts and roll into balls. Position the ball of fillings into the center of each pastry and wrap, roll in the all-purpose flour. Place the mooncake seam-side on the baking sheet. Spray with water and bake in the preheated oven for 8 minutes. Remove from the oven and reduce the temperature to 150°C.
- Brush with the beaten egg yolk, apply more to the top, return to the oven, bake until golden brown for 15 minutes, and cool completely.

MAPLE NUTS MOONCAKES

Preparation Time: 40 mins.

Cooking Time: 40 mins.

Servings: 12

Ingredients:

- 120 g. cake flour (all-purpose flour)
- ¼ c. golden syrup

- 2 tbsp. vegetable oil
- ½ tsp. lye water
- 1 ½ c. mixed nuts, preferably roasted
- ½ c. maple syrup
- ½ tsp. cinnamon
- ½ tsp. kosher salt
- Egg wash
- 1 egg
- Water splash

Directions:

- To make the mooncake dough. Mix the golden syrup, lye water, and vegetable oil in a medium-sized bowl. Difficult to get it smooth but try.
- Add your flour and stir until you get a thick dough; once all the flour has been completely added, knead until the dough is smooth but a bit very sticky and tightly and place in the fridge for 30 minutes minimum.

For the Maple Nut Filling:

- While waiting for the dough, prepare your filling following these steps. Add nuts, maple syrup, cinnamon, and salt into a blender and blend until it becomes a sticky mixture. The filling should be self-holding. Share the filling into 12 and roll into balls
- Prepare the oven at $175°C$ and bake
- Divide the mooncake dough into 12 portions. Wrap the mooncake around the filling. Turn to your baking tray and put it in the oven for 8 minutes.
- Make an egg wash, remove the mooncakes from the oven, and cool for 10 minutes. Apply the egg wash with a pastry brush and return the mooncake to the oven for 10-12 minutes until they turn golden yellow. Cool completely.

SUSHI WHITE MOONCAKES

Preparation Time: 1 hr.

Cooking Time: 20 mins.

Servings: 20

Ingredients:

- 150 g. Cake Flour
- 50 g. Bread flour

- 20 g. White sugar
- 90 ml. Water
- 50 ml. Vegetable oil

For the Filling:

- 180 g. cake flour
- 90 ml. Vegetable oil.
- 600 g. Tsuba-an.

Directions:

- Combine the ingredients to make the dough for the outside. Do the same with the 1¼ Tsubu-an ingredients to prepare the filling.
- Cover with plastic wrap keeps for 30 minutes in the fridge. Share both dough and fillings into 20 equal portions, and wrap them up, allowing them to rest for 10 mins at room temperature.
- Adjust the exterior dough with a rolling pin to your desired shape and cover them to rest for 15 mins at room temperature.
- Adjust with the rolling pin again, leave the seams facing upwards, end together, gently remove the dough by hand into a circle, and place the Anko on top.
- Bake at 180°C for 15 minutes. Take them out and bake for another 4 mins.

DRIED FRUIT AND NUTTY MOONCAKES

Preparation Time: 45 mins.

Cooking Time: 20 mins.

Servings: 16

Ingredients:

- 500 g. Plain flour
- 340 g. Sugar syrup
- 100 g. peanut oil
- 2 tsp. Alkaline water
- 80 g. Walnut, toasted and grinded
- 80 g. Silver almond toasted and grinded
- 60 g. toasted melon seeds
- 60 g. toasted pine nut
- 60 g. toasted white sesame
- 60 g. Dried cranberry, cut into small pieces
- 60 g. Dried Apricot cut to small pieces
- 60 g. Dried Mango cut into small pieces
- 60 g. Raisins, cut into small pieces
- 60 g. Prunes cut into small pieces
- 2 tbsp. Sugar
- 100 g. Kao fen
- ½ tsp. Salt
- 3 tbsp. Apricot Jam
- 2 ½ tbsp. Canola oil
- 6 tbsp. Water

Directions:

- Combine and mix all the ingredients.
- Mix well and share into 12 pieces ball shape.
- Dust some plain flour on a table and knead dough A until smooth.
- Wrap the filling with the soft dough, dust some plain flour, and place it inside the mold.
- Bake at 190°C for 10 minutes in the oven. Cool.
- Remove and brush some glaze on the mooncake.

SAVORY PREPARATION PORK MOONCAKES

Preparation Time: 2 hrs.

Cooking Time: 25 mins.

Servings: 24

Ingredients:

- 1 pound ground pork
- ¼ c. sugar
- 2 tbsp. honey
- 2 tbsp. Shaoxing wine
- 1 tsp. salt
- 1 tbsp. light soy sauce
- 1 tsp. ginger powder
- ½ tsp. garlic powder
- 1 scallion
- 1 egg
- ¼ c. toasted sesame

For the Soft Dough:

- 2 ¼ c. all-purpose flour
- 2 ½ tsp. sugar
- ⅓ c. lard
- ½ c. water

For the Pastry Dough:

- 1 ½ c. all-purpose flour
- ½ c. lard

Directions:

- Prepare meat filling by mixing the ingredients. Cover and keep aside.
- Prepare the soft dough, add the flour, sugar, and lard, and mix until thoroughly combined.
- Prepare pastry dough to combine the flour and lard. Also, knead to form the dough ball and keep it in the fridge for 20 minutes.
- Dive the pastry dough and the soft dough into 24 pieces.

- Wrap the pastry dough at the center of the soft dough.
- Roll into a disc with the rolling pin. Add one tbsp. of the meat fillings to the center of the disc and seal tightly.
- Press the dough shape into the mooncake shape, place it on the baking sheet. Preheat the oven at 400°C, place the baking sheet in the middle of the oven and brush the cakes with egg wash.
- Sprinkle the top with sesame seeds and bake for 25minutes until the cake turns a golden color.

CHAPTER 5: JAPANESE MOONCAKES RECIPE

MOCHI MOONCAKES

Preparation Time: 15 mins.

Cooking Time: 15 mins.

Servings: 20

Ingredients:

- 600 g. Icing sugar
- 225 g. Cooked rice flour
- 120 g. lard
- 8 oz. water
- Pandan flavor/banana essence

Directions:

- Sift the rice flour and icing sugar well mixed in a large mixing bowl.
- Form a well in the middle of the flour, insert the lard, water, and mix thoroughly and set aside for 20 minutes.
- Share the dough into 50 g. each and wrap with filling.
- Press mooncake into molds.

MATCHA SNOW WHITE MOONCAKES

Preparation Time: 1 hr.

Cooking Time: 40 mins.

Servings: 12

Ingredients:

- 40 g. glutinous rice flour
- 35 g. rice flour
- 15 g. wheat starch
- ½ tsp. matcha powder (Japanese green tea powder)
- 40 g. icing sugar
- 145 g. milk
- 15 g. cooking oil

Directions:

- Mix glutinous rice, rice flour, wheat starch, matcha powder, and icing sugar. Add cooking oil, milk and mix thoroughly. Sift the mixture into a heat resistance pan.
- Steam under moderate heat for 25 minutes.
- Stir until it becomes smooth while hot. Put aside to slightly cool, then wrap and cool for 30 mins.
- Stir-fry 1 tbsp. of glutinous rice flour, subject to moderate heat for 5 minutes.
- Divide the Matcha bean paste into ten portions.
- Divide snow skin into ten portions.
- Adjust snow skin into a flat shape, top with filling, then fully wrap the filling with snow skin. Lightly coat with hand-coating flour, then use the mooncake mold to print patterns.
- Chill before serving (1-hour minimum).

LYCHEE MARTINI SNOW SKIN MOONCAKES

Preparation Time: 30 mins.

Cooking Time: 30 mins.

Servings: 12

Ingredients:

For the Lychee-White Bean Paste Filling:

- 7 oz. dried lima beans or white beans of your choice
- One ¼ c. syrup from canned lychee
- ¼ tsp. kosher salt

For the Mooncake Wrapper:

- ¾ c. unsweetened full-fat coconut milk
- 1 tbsp. vegetable oil
- 1–2 tsp. rosewater
- ⅓ c. packed powdered sugar
- ⅓ c. sweet rice flour (also labelled mochiko or glutinous rice flour)
- ¼ c. rice flour
- 3 tbsp. tapioca flour
- ¼ c. strawberry or raspberry powder (optional)

Directions:

- Rinse white beans well and place in a large container with excess water overnight until the skin peels off and is easily removed. When the beans are soaked, remove the skin and discard.
- Boil the beans for 2 mins until foam appears, then drain off the water. Replace the water and boil the beans until its softened.
- Drain the beans and blend them, adding some lychee syrup. Combine the beans paste obtained, lychee syrup, and salt and mix well to get a liquid soupy.
- For the wrapper, Combine coconut milk and vegetable oil in a cup. Whisk in a separate bowl glutinous rice flour, icing sugar, rice flour, and tapioca flour. Pour the coconut milk into the flour mixture and beat until well-combined mixture. Cook over moderate heat with constant stirring until the moisture completely evaporates and takes a form that can be molded.
- Sieve the batter into a clean heatproof bowl. Steam the content for 25-30 minutes with constant stirring until it becomes jelly-like solid. Transfer the dough to parchment paper on a flat surface.
- Knead until the dough is soft while still hot. Wrap the dough in plastic wrap and chill for about 3 hours. Insert a piece of lychee into each filling scoop and gently shape the fillings into balls.
- Wrap the dough around the filling. Dust the mooncake mold and ball well with tapioca. Insert the dough ball and press firmly to achieve the mooncake's shape.

MUNG BEAN MOONCAKES

Preparation Time: 1 hr.

Cooking Time: 1 hr.

Servings: 12

Ingredients:

- 200 g. split mung beans
- 50 g. sugar
- ⅛ tsp. salt
- 50 g. oil plus more
- 20 g. corn starch
- Red bean paste, for filling

Directions:

- Soak the mung Beans (4 hours minimum).
- Cook until it becomes soft, drain, and you can form a paste from it. Blend.
- Cook again, this time adding cooking oil, sugar, and salt until the bean paste started leaving the side of the paste.
- Transfer to another plate and spread to completely cool. Divide the mung bean paste and the double sha fillings into 12 portions each.
- Place the dough sha fillings in the middle and wrap. Use the mold and press out of the mold and let them chill in the refrigerator for a minimum of one hour.

KIWI FRUIT MOONCAKES

Preparation Time: 30 mins.

Cooking Time: 10 mins.

Servings: 6

Ingredients:

- 200 ml. Water
- 2 ½ tsp. Sugar
- 1 Pandan leaf
- 1 tsp. agar powder (fresh)
- 3 tbsp. freshly prepared milk
- One drop of red and egg yellow coloring
- 380 ml. Water
- 3 ½ tbsp. Sugar

- 2 Pandan leaves
- 1 ¾ tsp. Agar agar powder
- 1 ½ Green kiwi fruits
- 1 ½ gold kiwi fruits
- 5-8 red cherries

Directions:

- Combine the water, sugar, agar-agar powder, and pandan leaf in one pot at moderate heat. Use a hand whisk to stir until liquid boils. Remove the pandan leaf and add 3 tbsp. of fresh milk and stir.
- Share liquid into two parts and add two drops of cherry red and egg yellow coloring into each portion and stir well.
- Slash red cherries, green and gold kiwifruits into cube shapes and keep one side
- Combine the water(380g), sugar, agar-agar powder, and pandan leaf in one pot at moderate heat. Use a hand whisk to stir until liquid boils. Remove pandan leaf, add kiwifruits and cherries into the mixture, remove the heat, and stir.
- Remove jellies mold from the refrigerator and add the kiwi fruit mixture. Scoop the kiwifruits into each space and keep them in the refrigerator.

PIGGY SNOW SKIN MOONCAKES

Preparation Time: 1 hr.

Cooking Time: 40 mins.

Servings: 12

Ingredients:

- 150 g. Gao Fen (cooked glutinous rice flour)
- 150 g. Icing Sugar
- 50 g. Shortening
- 180 g. cold water
- A little Wilton pink gel food coloring
- Mooncake filling

Directions:

- Mix Sift Gao Fen and icing sugar together in a bowl.
- Add shortening to the mixture and combine. Add pink coloured water slowly to the mixture until you can knead.
- Flatten dough. Take a little dough, form an oval shape for the piggy's nose, use a straw to make two holes.
- Take the small dough, mould it into two ovals for piggy's ears. Use chocolate chips for piggy's eyes and little dough rolled out for piggy's tail.

FUZHOU DOU YONG MOONCAKES

Preparation Time: 20 mins.

Cooking Time: 20 mins.

Servings: 10

Ingredients:

For the Mochi Dough:

- 80 g. glutinous rice flour
- 20 g. wheat starch
- 2 ½ tbsp. Sugar
- ½ tsp. banana essence
- 150 ml. water
- 2 tbsp. corn oil

For the Pastry Dough:

- 120 g. all-purpose flour
- 15 g. icing sugar
- 45 g. butter, melted
- 70 ml. cold water

Directions:

- Mix the Mochi dough without water, rub butter and dry ingredients, blend butter and dry ingredients still will be blended. Finally, add water to form a soft dough and knead till it is smooth and kept aside. Divide to 10 equal portions.
- Mix the Pastry dough till everything conforms together well and divide it into ten equal portions.
- Wrap the pastry dough into the Mochi dough. Seal and keep aside for 10 minutes.
- Transfer into the baking tray and bake at 180°C for about 20 minutes till a brown color is achieved.

JAPANESQUE GREEN TEA MOONCAKES

Preparation Time: 20 mins.

Cooking Time: 1 hr.

Servings: 10

Ingredients:

- 40 g. glutinous rice flour
- 35 g. rice flour
- 15 g. wheat starch
- ½ tsp. matcha powder (Japanese green tea powder)
- 40 g. icing sugar
- 145 g. milk
- 15 g. cooking oil
- 200 g. Matcha Mung Bean Paste

Directions:

- Mix the glutinous rice flour, wheat starch, matcha powder, and icing sugar. Mix milk and knead until smooth, add cooking oil, continue with the kneading until smooth.
- Sift the combination into a heat resistance pan. Steam under moderate heat for 25 minutes.
- Stir with a spatula while hot, then wrap and cool for 30 minutes. Stir fry 1 tbsp. rice flour in a dry pan over moderate heat and keep aside to cool.
- Divide Matcha mung and Matcha snow skin into 1o portions each, wrap the Matcha mung ball with snow skin, and then use a mold.
- Chill the cake for one hour for better texture before serving.

WARABI MOCHI MOONCAKES

Preparation Time: 10 mins.

Cooking Time: 15 mins.

Servings: 4

Ingredients:

- ¾ c. Warabiko (bracken starch) / tapioca starch
- ½ c. sugar
- 1 ¾ c. water
- ¼ c. kinako (Soybean flour)
- Brown sugar syrup

Directions:

- Get all ingredients set and splash some kinako on the baking board. Mix the Warabi Mochiko, sugar, and water and mix all in a medium pan.
- Boil the mixture. Reduce the heat and stir at a constant rate thoroughly for 10 minutes until the mixture is thick. Wait until it transforms to a clear color.
- Remove mochi from the heat and transfer to a baking sheet covered with (soybean flour). Splash and let it cool in the fridge for 20 minutes
- Take out of the refrigerator and slice into ¾ inch cube. Toss your warabi mochi with some kinako and serve.

CHIDORI MANJU MOONCAKES

Preparation Time: 1 hr.

Cooking Time: 10 mins.

Servings: 12

Ingredients:

- ½ c. brown sugar
- 3 tbsp. Water
- ½ tbsp. Baking powder
- ½ tsp. water
- 1 c. cake flour
- 8.5 oz. Anko

Directions:

- Gather all the ingredients. Combine water and brown sugar into a small saucepan. Dissolve the sugar over moderate heat.
- Transfer to a large bowl and cool. Wet your hand with a sprinkle of water and roll 12 balls of red bean paste 20g size.
- Mix baking powder and water. Combine with the cooled brown sugar mixture and mix all together. Sift all the flour, add to the brown sugar mixture, and mix well. Cover with plastic wrap and keep for 15 minutes. Transfer the dough to work surface and knead for 1-2minute
- Form a flat dough and wrap it around the red beanball. Cover the Manju with a wet towel to prevent drying and set up and steamer. Occupy the pot with 2 inches of water and allow the water to boil. Let the steaming process continue for up to 12 minutes; once the cooking is complete, cool.
- Wrap each Manju with a plastic wrap while still warm and enjoy!

VEGAN SNOW SKIN MOCHI MOONCAKES

Preparation Time: 1 hr.

Cooking Time: 30 mins.

Servings: 4

Ingredients:

For the Filling:

- 300 g. purple sweet potato
- ½ c. coconut cream
- ⅔ c. water
- ¼ c. coconut oil
- ⅓ c. sweetened coconut condensed milk
- 80 g. arrowroot starch.
- A pinch salt
- 1 tsp. sweet potato powder
- ½ tsp. blue butterfly pea powder

For the Wrapper:

- ⅓ c. arrowroot starch
- ⅔ c. rice flour
- ⅔ c. glutinous rice flour
- 100 g. maple syrup
- Almond milk
- ¼ c. coconut oil, melted
- ¼ tsp. matcha green tea for natural colouring
- A pinch pink pitaya for natural colouring

Directions:

- Steam for 15-20 mins already peeled and chopped potatoes of about 300g in a large pot.
- Make a paste from the cooked potato by blending, covering with a plastic wrap, and refrigerating.
- Combine all the ingredients, glutinous rice, rice flour, arrowroot starch to a large heat-safe bowl and mix well. Add almond milk, maple syrup, and melted coconut oil for complete mixing.
- Knead the dough with hands and cool for 1 hour.
- Cook about 35g rice flour in a small pan for stirring constantly4-5 mins until a slightly yellow color is seen.
- Cool the fillings and weigh 12 g, roll into balls, wrap, and place in the fridge
- Add ¼ tsp. matcha powder to half of the cooled wrapper dough and add a pinch of pitaya powder to the other half.
- Take 12 g of white wrapper dough and wrap it into balls. Keep the fillings in the center of the wrapper and wrap.
- Insert the mooncakes into the mold and mold.

KETO MOONCAKES

Preparation Time: 15 mins.

Cooking Time: 20 mins.

Servings: 3

Ingredients:

- Whole psyllium husk
- 6 salted egg yolk
- 50 g. butter
- 20 g. melon seed
- 50 g. water
- 30 g. erythritol
- 70 g. coconut flour
- ½ tsp. salt
- 4 g. xanthan gum
- Almond flour
- 50 g. Macadamia
- 16 g. pine nut
- 100 g. peanut
- 200 g. allulose
- 30 g. butter

Directions:

- Set the oven to (190°C). Prepare all the ingredients for filling. Add enough peanut butter and separate into a 30-g. Cluster each. Our goal is to form a dough ball.

- Combine all the ingredients in a bowl to prepare the dough.
- Use your hand to knead the dough. Flatten with your hand, put the filling on top of one, and cover with the second flattened dough.
- Spray the mooncake press with spray.
- Insert dough ball in the mold and shape into a mooncake with an imprint on the top.
- Place the dough on a baking sheet in the middle of the oven and bake for 5 minutes.
- Let the mooncake cool for 10 minutes. Beat egg yolk with a pinch of some water and brush the cake with soft bristles. Return the baking sheet into the oven and bake over another 10 mins to achieve a golden-brown nature.
- Remove from the oven, cool for 5 minutes, and transfer them into the cooling rack for complete cooling.
- Do not eat the mooncakes the same day you baked them.

WAGASHI MOONCAKES

Preparation Time: 30 mins.

Cooking Time: 2 hrs.

Servings:

Ingredients:

- 350 g. dried white beans
- 300 g. white sugar
- Water

Directions:

- Clean and soak white beans overnight. Peel the skin.
- Keep the beans in a pot. Add 1 inch of cold water sufficient to cover the beans.
- Remove scum and cook the beans.
- Boil the water.
- Blend the beans into a paste with the use of a stick blender. Use a sieve to strain the beans and form a wet paste.
- Add sugar and cook until the bean paste thickens. Remove from the pot and cool.

PANDAN SPIRAL MOONCAKES

Preparation Time: 3 hrs.

Cooking Time: 30 min

Servings: 10-12

Ingredients:

For the Filling:

- 400-500 g. taro root
- A pinch of salt

For the Moon Cake Dough:

- 200 g. bleached cake flour (water dough)
- 200 g. confectioners' sugar
- A pinch of salt
- 80 g. cold unsalted butter
- 180 g. bleached cake flour (oil dough)
- A pinch of salt
- 90 g. oil
- ½ tsp. pandan essence

Directions:

- Rinse and peel taro. Cut into equal 300g. Boil the taro pieces in a pot of salted water. Boil until the water the taro becomes soft (25 mins).
- Separate the taro from the water and make a thick paste rollable into balls. Roll into 20 balls.
- Prepare the water dough by sifting 200g flour, confectioners' sugar, and salt in a large bowl.
- Cut 80 g cold butter to the flour mixture using a blender till the mixture looks like breadcrumbs.
- Add 80g water and mix to form a softball that does not stick to your hand. Make the oil dough by sifting 180 g of flour and salt.
- Create a deep well in the center of the flour and add 90g oil and pandan essence. Mix. Cover and set aside for 20 minutes. Preheat the oven to 180 C.
- Share the water and oil dough equally in ten different places. Adjust using a pastry cutter, sharp knife.
- Wrap the filling and pinch to seal. Placed the sealed side down on lined and bake for 30 minutes until the top and bottoms are a light golden brown.

SWEET POTATO MOONCAKES

Preparation Time: 15 mins.

Cooking Time: 20 mins.

Servings: 4

Ingredients:

- Three sweet potatoes
- 4 to 6 tbsp. rice flour
- ¼ tsp. salt
- Powdered sugar to taste (optional)
- 2 tbsp. melted butter cooled

Directions:

- Clean and scrub the sweet potatoes. Boil under low heat and cover the pot, simmer for about 20 mins until it is soft.
- Cool the sweet potatoes. After then, toast the rice flour in a pan until browned and cool.
- Peel the sweet potato and mash. Make 2 c. of mashed potato, add salt and rice flour to the sweet potato. Mix lightly but thoroughly but avoid over mixing.
- Form the mixture into small balls. Serve the potato tea cakes with hot tea.
- Press each ball into the mold, then use the handle to release.

JELLY WITH COCONUT MOONCAKES

Preparation Time: 30 mins.

Cooking Time: 10 mins.

Servings:

Ingredients:

For the Jelly:

- 5 c. pandan water blended with 2 c. of shredded pandan leaves
- 20 g. agar-agar powder
- ¾ c. sugar
- 30 g. edible flowers

For the Coconut Toppings:

- 2 ½ c. coconut milk
- 30 g. rice flour
- 10 g. agar-agar powder
- 1 tsp. salt
- 30 g. jasmine flowers

Directions:

- Mix the pandan water and agar-agar powder, boil.
- Add sugar, stir to dissolve. Pour mixture into a bottle or jar, add flowers. Cool it
- Combine the coconut milk, rice flour, agar-agar powder, and salt and boil the mixture. Cool it and pour it over the jelly mixture. Leave to set, then top with jasmine. Cover and refrigerate it overnight.
- Remove the jasmine flower.

MUNG BEAN MOONCAKES

Preparation Time: 10 mins.

Cooking Time: 60 mins.

Servings: 6

Ingredients:

- 200 g. split mung beans, peeled
- 100 g. caster sugar
- 80 ml. coconut milk
- 70 ml. vegetable oil
- ⅛ tsp. salt
- 1 ½ tbsp. wheat starch

Directions:

- Wash mung beans and soak for at least four hours.
- Put the mung beans into a large shallow pan with water. Allow the beans to continue absorbing water along the cooking process. Steam in a wok over a high heat medium for about 25 to 30 mins until it becomes solid.
- Filter the beans out and rem0ove the excess water, and you will get a very smooth puree.
- Transfer the puree into a frypan. Add sugar, coconut milk, oil, and salt. Mix well and cook over a high heat medium until the water evaporates and is reduced by two-third. Separate the wheat flour in batches and stir to combine well in each phase.
- Reduce the heat and constantly stir about 30 to 35 minutes and simmer until thicken and allow to cool completely.
- Divide into portions and shape into balls. Make mung bean filling ahead, wrap it, and store it in the fridge.

TSUKIMI MOONCAKES

Preparation Time: 30 mins.

Cooking Time: 30 mins.

Servings: 15

Ingredients:

- 3 ½ oz. dangoko (Japanese rice dumpling flour)
- ⅔ c. water
- One slice squash/pumpkin (kabocha)

Directions:

- Gather all the ingredients. Boil Dango on low heat a big pot of water.
- Steam a thin slice of kabocha squash for 13-15 minutes (depending on thickness, the cooking Time differs). Try to shake it with a skewer, and if it enters quickly, it is done. Transfer with a spoon and peel. Mash and set aside.
- Add Dango to a bowl. Stir with water a little bit a Time until the danger starts to stick together and becomes clumps.
- Form a ball from the dough prepared and share into eight different portions, then divide each piece into two balls.
- Make two yellow balls, prepare 30 g. of dough, and mix in 2 tsp. mashed kabocha. Bring the kabocha and dough together well. Shape to a nice smooth round ball, so in total, there are two yellow balls and 15 white balls.
- Boil water in the pot and gently drop each ball into the pot. Stir the balls occasionally, so they don't stick on the bottom of the pot. Dango will float when fully cooked, then cook for an additional 1-2 minutes and transfer to iced water for cooling. Transfer to the tray.

TAIYAKI MOONCAKES

Preparation Time: 10 mins.

Cooking Time: 5 mins.

Servings: 6-7

Ingredients:

- 170 g. butter
- 65 g. light brown sugar
- 100 g. egg
- 240 g. cake flour
- 6 g. baking powder
- 155 g. warm milk
- 10 g. honey
- 6 g. light soy sauce
- 4 g. vanilla extract
- Store-bought/ locally made Red Bean Paste

Directions:

For the Adzuki Beans Paste:

- Pressure cooks the adzuki beans with the water for 1 hour, topping off the water as it reduces. When the beans are cooking, puree them in a blender until you achieve a smooth coarse texture.
- Return the bean to the cooking pan and add enough water to sticky the paste.
- Add sugar and cook the bean with sugar with constant stirring until the sugar fully dissolves. Cool the paste until you can touch it with your bare hands.
- Sieve to get a finer paste and shape the paste so that it will contain the fish-shaped taiyaki.
- Mix milk, honey, soy sauce, and vanilla extract and keep the cream and the butter together with sugar, one egg, half flour, then milk, then the other half flour.
- With the aid of a squeeze bottle, squeeze a pool of batter into the body. Insert the red bean at the middle of the taiyaki.
- Check the readiness of each side and if not done, continue with the grilling at intervals until they are golden brown.
- Serve while warm and crunchy.

CLIPPER EARL MOONCAKES

Preparation Time: 30 mins.

Cooking Time: 30 mins.

Servings: 10

Ingredients:

- 15 tbsp. Clipper Earl Grey Dried Tea leaves
- 30 g. Earl Grey Tea
- 100 g. Kou Fen
- 50 g. Caster Sugar
- 30 g. Salted Butter
- 90 g. Chilled Ice-cream Soda
- 200 g. White Lotus Paste
- 20 g. Diced Dried Apricot

Directions:

- Mix 1.5 tbsp. of Clipper Earl Grey Leaves with a half c. of boiling water. Keep aside for cooling and infusion.
- Add sugar to sifted Kou fou and stir. Include softened butter and mix with the back of a spoon to obtain a crumbly mixture.

- Add in the chilled Soda and Earl Grey Tea and mix slowly until the liquid is absorbed. Knead into the soft, smooth dough while getting the filling ready.
- Drain the tea leaves, then add to the white lotus paste. Mix thoroughly with hand and share the filling to each ball.
- Wrap the lotus filling inside the flattened dough and cover it up.
- Dust the mooncake mold firmly. Knock to unmold the mooncake.

RICE MOONCAKES

Preparation Time: 1 hr. 20 mins.

Cooking Time: 40 mins.

Servings: 12

Ingredients:

For the Mooncake Dough:

- Rice Flour
- Glutinous Rice Flour
- Honey- You can also use corn syrupy or maltose as a substitute.
- Corn oil
- Boiling Water

For the Oreo (or Strawberry Jam) Cream Cheese Filling:

- Oreo Cookies (Strawberry Jam as a substitute)
- Cream Cheese
- Granulated Sugar

Directions:

- Add rice flour to a frypan. Fry continuously under moderate heat for 5 to 10 minutes. Watch to turn off the heat when the flour turns brownish and transfer to a separate bowl.
- Add corn oil, honey, and boiling water to the cooked flour. Mix well with a spatula. Knead the dough for some Times more than five minutes until smooth.
- Divide the dough into three equal portions of different colorants.
- Make the Oreo or Strawberry Jam Cream Cheese Filling.
- Remove the cookies cream fillings from Oreos. Blend the cookies with a blender. Add the cookies crumble, cream crumbles, cream cheese, and sugar in a bowl. The mix will share into 20g and rolled into balls. Refrigerate for 20 minutes.
- Adjust the cake and place the moon cake in the mold. Press the mold and make a mooncake pattern out of it—Bake in 5 minutes in the oven for 365F.

RED BEAN BUN MOONCAKES

Preparation Time: 20 mins.

Cooking Time: 15 mins.

Servings: 4

Ingredients:

- 340 g. High-gluten flour
- 60 g. low-gluten flour
- 35 g. Caster sugar
- 30 g. Milk powder
- 5 g. Salt
- 30 g. Butter
- 250 g. Water
- 5 g. instant dry yeast
- 48 g. red bean paste
- Black Sesame

Directions:

- Combine the dough ingredients in the mixer and knead. Cover the dough and ferment it.
- Put it into the basin and cover it with plastic wrap to rise and increase in size.
- When the dough is ready, remove and divide it into 12 equal parts. Use the Red bean paste store-bought or prepared and add it as a filling, divide it into 12 portions and knead round and keep aside.
- When the buns double up, spray a little water and a little black sesame and keep it in the preheated oven for baking for about 18 minutes.

SHIROAN MOONCAKES

Preparation Time: 30 mins.

Cooking Time: 2 hrs.

Servings: 1

Ingredients:

- 7 oz dried lima beans
- ¾ c. sugar
- ½ sea salt

Directions:

- Gather all ingredients.
- Soak rinsed lima inside plenty of water overnight (8-12 hours), skin with your fingers.
- Prepare the beans in a pot, add enough water to cover it, and boil for 2 minutes until you start noticing foam. Remove the water and add another cold water to it. Heat for close to 2 hours until the beans are soft. Using a pressure cooker makes it faster. Always be sure that water covers up the bean during cooking.
- Make a paste from the cooked bean. Add sugar and salt. Mix well to combine.
- Lower the heat, allow the sugar to dissolve. The paste will become liquid.
- Heat and let the moisture evaporate from the mixture under medium heat for roughly 15-20 minutes. Monitor paste to prevent it from burning.
- The dough is completely cooked when you can draw the line at the bottom of the pot. Paste continues to evaporate as it cools down.

CONCLUSION

If you made it this far to this part of this cookbook, then I believe you have been well equipped with a full-stack knowledge of making different Mooncakes. All their recipes were described in a well-structured and organized manner.

Your level of expertise does not matter. You can easily follow up the instructional steps in this book and try out your version of every individual type of Mooncakes found in this book.

The recipes are the best popular ones found around the world, and in some cases where the recipes might be difficult to get in a given location, other ingredients that are useful as substitutes are stated beside them to get you the appropriate taste of an individual

All the techniques and steps towards the preparation of the delicious Mooncake are highlighted and can upgrade your kitchen skills to the next level

Every individual Mooncake recipe contains adequate nutrients, combining vitamins and minerals. These food classes boost the digestive system's performance because they are heavily loaded with high fiber content, thus reducing constipation. This primarily helps the liver breakdown the harmful effects of substances that are capable of poising the body system

Some Mooncake recipes act as antioxidants and increase the rate of fat loss in the body. Others are full of proteins and nutrients that repair the body's cells. This, in turn, helps weight loss and regulates the blood sugar level.

Conclusively, try following the instruction steps strictly to get the replica of the Mooncakes. However, there are some ingredients you might need to add more or less, depending on your personal preference.

Enjoy adding a bulk of experience to your kitchen skills by trying to make your homemade version of the Mooncake

Thank you!

Made in the USA
Monee, IL
18 February 2022